[TWENTY THESES ON POLITICS]

A Book in the Series

LATIN AMERICA IN TRANSLATION / EN TRADUCCIÓN / EM TRADUÇÃO

Sponsored by the Duke–University of North Carolina Program
in Latin American Studies

TWENTY
THESES
ON
POLITICS

ENRIQUE
DUSSEL

TRANSLATED
BY
GEORGE
CICCARIELLO-MAHER

FOREWORD
BY
EDUARDO
MENDIETA

DUKE
UNIVERSITY
PRESS

DURHAM
AND
LONDON
2008

PRINTED

IN THE

UNITED STATES

OF AMERICA

ON ACID-FREE

PAPER ∞

DESIGNED BY

JENNIFER HILL

TYPESET IN

ADOBE JENSON PRO

BY KEYSTONE

TYPESETTING, INC.

LIBRARY

OF CONGRESS

CATALOGING-IN-

PUBLICATION

DATA APPEAR

ON THE

LAST PRINTED

PAGE OF

THIS BOOK.

Contents

Part Two:

THE CRITICAL TRANSFORMATION OF THE POLITICAL:

TOWARD THE NEW POLITICAL ORDER

THE LIBERATION OF POLITICS: ALTERITY, SOLIDARITY, LIBERATION
Eduardo Mendieta

Historical periods are sometimes referred to by descriptive names such as the age of reason, the age of faith, the age of revolutions, the age of totalitarianism, the age of global wars, and so on. The prophets of neoliberal globalization, with their vision skewed by the shadow of events barely past, undoubtedly would like to call our times "the age of the abolition of politics." Globalization is an ideology that would have the world surrender to a blind technological and economic drive. Globalization is a fetishizing way to represent for others— those who can't represent themselves, as Marx and Spivak claimed—the present state of humanity primarily because it subordinates the political to the economic and the economic to the technological. The maps of globalization, drawn by the master cartographers of the Pentagon, the World Bank, the Deutsche Bank, Microsoft, and the International Monetary Fund, are utopias in which the space of the political is violently colonized and then abolished by monetary and legalistic imperatives. The political, or rather the spheres of the political, as Enrique Dussel points out in this book, is assimilated and subordinated to the management of investments, technological modernizations, and budgetary calculations. The political is thus translated into an algorithm that maximizes profits and returns on investments while minimizing costs by passing them off to future generations.

This mistranslation that legitimates the massive private accumulation of collective wealth, which is proportionally matched by generalized dispossession and impoverishment, is but an alchemy that turns what is most fundamentally human—the political—into the most anti-human: thus the necrophilic love of profit—politics as the expression of the lust for and the will to live off the human—turns into necropolitics (to use that most apropos expression by Achille Mbembe). The abolition of the political is thus the negation of human life, not just as naked existence but as collective, communitarian, dialogical, communicative freedom. Without others, without the other, there is neither ethics nor politics. Without others, without the other, there is no politics as the horizon of the possible—the possibility of continued existence. It is this continued existence as coexistence, as surviving and flourishing with others, that is the source of the political. It is this politics that is being abolished by the profiteers of global war and neoliberal pillage. Against this necropolitics of neoliberal globalization, a politics of liberation—a politics of life with others and for others—is proclaimed from below. It is this politics of life, and for life, that proclaims that politics is the proper vocation of the human being. It is this proclamation from below, from the victims of capitalism, imperialism, ecocide, and genocide, that gives us reason to pause and to affirm that ours will be the age of global politics, the age of the politics of alterity. Enrique Dussel's *Twenty Theses on Politics*, originally published in Spanish in 2006, is the manifesto of this politics of alterity, a politics of life and for life, a politics from the underside of necrophilic globalization.

While this manifesto is brief, and almost telegraphic in its presentation, it is neither simple nor a mere exercise in oracular proclamation. Behind every paragraph stands decades of philosophical work as well as hundreds of pages of philosophical analysis. Dussel is unquestionably the best-known living philosopher from Latin America, and surely he is to have the most lasting effect on planetary thinking. His work, since its earliest formulations in the 1950s and 1960s, was avowedly articulated as a philosophy of liberation. In 1975 he published *Philosophy of Liberation*, which summarized a decade of work on what at the time he called a "deconstruction of ethics" and "an ethics of Latin American liberation." *Philosophy of Liberation* articulated not just a project for the liberation of philosophy but also an ethics and politics of liberation. Through the late 1970s and early 1980s, Dussel dedicated himself to a reconstruction of Karl Marx's philosophical itinerary from that of a young Hegelian to a mature critic of political economy. This decade of philological, archival, and exegetical work at the Marx-Lenin Institute in Moscow yielded what some have called the most important reconstructive readings of Marx's political economy to be done in the last quarter of the twentieth century. Just as it was not possible to read Marx during the 1960s without the aid of Rosdolsky, Lukács, and Marcuse, now it is no longer possible to go back to *Capital* without the aid of Dussel's three volumes on Marx's manuscripts and drafts of that work. Yet Dussel's work is not produced primarily in library halls or in the solitary reading rooms of archives and institutes; rather, it emerges from his pedagogy across the Americas and the world and from his continued and dizzying dialogues, debates, and encounters with other philosophers. Perhaps one of his most notorious encounters was with Karl-Otto Apel in a decade-long dialogue on the relationship between Dussel's proposal for an ethics of liberation and Apel's version of discourse ethics.

Two decades after his *Philosophy of Liberation* and his numerous books on Marx, Latin American philosophy, and contemporary philosophy, Dussel published one of his most important works, *Ethics of Liberation in the Age of Globalization and Exclusion*. This volume synthesized Dussel's unique reading of Emmanuel Levinas's ethics of alterity, with Dussel's own Schellingian reading of Marx (which affirms that Marx's notion of "living-labor" is the central category in *Capital*) and with his new appreciation of procedural formalism, which he gained through his debates with Karl-Otto Apel. *Ethics of Liberation* is a strikingly original, prodigiously documented, staggeringly systematic and coherent work of moral philosophy, and it is, furthermore, unusual in its historical scope. The book opens disarmingly with an introduction subtitled "Global History of Ethicities," which given its length could easily have been printed as a separate book with the title "A World History of Ethical Systems." The rest of the book is divided into two parts: "Foundations of Ethics" and "Ethical Critique, Anti-Hegemonic Validity, and the Praxis of Liberation." *Ethics of Liberation* is probably one of the most extensive, detailed, and well-argued systematic articulations of the principles of moral reasoning that is at the same time linked to a cosmopolitan, decolonized, post-occidentalist history of moral philosophy.

Enrique Dussel's ethics of liberation argues that ethics has at its foundation a material moment—that is, it has to do with corporeal need. Ethics is grounded in practical truth, namely survival. But simultaneously it is entwined with the moments of what Dussel calls intersubjective validity and feasibility. The ethical has to do with our relations to others, and through those relations, our relations to ourselves, and thus it entails a series of principles of intersubjective solicitude and respect. At the same time, the aim of ethical acts must be within the horizon of the possible. The ethical is related to feasibility; what can be properly described as ethical is part and parcel of a possible act or action.

Yet every positive and normative description of the foundations of ethics (meant in the Kantian sense of offering both a point of departure and a "justification") also entails the critique of them. Every ethical system, or *Sittlichkeit*, is always already incomplete and in violation of its own assumptions and normative commitments. Thus, Dussel devotes the second part of *Ethics of Liberation* to an analysis of what he calls negative ethics. The first principle of negative, or critical, ethics demands that we critique every ethical system that entails the production of certain victims. Ethical critique commands that we look at our ethical system from the location of its specific victims. Every ethical system cannot but exclude some who are affected by the very performance of that system's goals and expectations. Thus anti-hegemonic ethical critique demands that we critique the system of intersubjective validity from the perspective of the voice of those who are not heard and the claims of those who are intentionally or unintentionally excluded from our ethical deliberations. Finally, the praxis of liberation commands that we engage in the processes of transformation of our ethical system so as to allow for the coexistence of those the system has made into victims. There is no ethics if there is no praxis of liberation, and only those who engage in such a praxis of liberation can be granted the name of having sought after "goodness." Thus ethical goodness synergizes practical truth, intersubjective validity, and feasibility as enacted from the locus of the victims of each and every ethical system.

The overview given above is indispensable for a proper appreciation of the disarming succinctness and terseness of this volume. Behind *Twenty Theses on Politics* are three hefty volumes in a set titled *Politics of Liberation*. The first volume, which was published 2007 under the title *Política de la liberación:*

Historia Mundial y Crítica, is a global and critical history of political philosophy. Like the introduction to *Ethics of Liberation*, the first volume of *Politics of Liberation* offers a critical, decolonized, and post-occidentalist history of political philosophy which, as Dussel notes in his introduction, seeks to "de-structure" and "re-structure" seven major limitations or limits. A global or planetary history of political philosophy must seek to overcome the skewing and refracting influences first, of Hellenism; second, of occidentalism; and third, of Eurocentrism. As an evident consequence of these three limitations, the fourth limit is the privileging of a certain periodization of world history. The fifth limitation to overcome in any political philosophy with pretensions to planetary relevance is a fallacious and obfuscating secularism that misrepresents not only so-called Western culture but also its putative others. The sixth limitation to overcome is a hubristic theoretical and mental colonization that disowns and suppresses the political-philosophical contributions of marginalized societies. Seventh, and finally, Dussel urges in this *Politics of Liberation* that a decolonized, decolonizing, and planetary political philosophy must aim to denounce and correct the systematic exclusion of the Americas from the sociological, political, and philosophical narratives of the emergence of modernity. Volumes two and three, respectively titled *Politics of Liberation: Architectonic* and *Politics of Liberation: Critique*, are scheduled for publication in 2008 and 2009, respectively. In addition to the first volume of *Politics of Liberation*, Dussel published in 2007 a collection of his essays entitled *Hacia una filosofía política crítica*. This compilation of some twenty essays produced since the publication of his *Ethics of Liberation* anticipates and elaborates aspects of the *Politics*.

Although *Twenty Theses on Politics* is a synthesis and a summary of the three volumes of *Politics of Liberation* it neither duplicates them nor offers their theoretical density and presentation as a monumental work of scholarly analysis and cosmopolitan scope. What *Twenty Theses on Politics* does do, however, is to anticipate the general structure of the three-volume *Politics of Liberation*. The first part of *Twenty Theses* concerns the "prevailing political order," for which Dussel lays out the positive description of the three normative principles of politics: the material principle, the formal or normative principle, and the principles of feasibility. Politics concerns the preservation, enhancement, and continuation of the life of the political community—the people. But it also concerns in an originary and simultaneous way the principles of communal recognition and political delegation, as well as the principles of political realization and actualization. The second part of *Twenty Theses* is devoted to the development of the critical principles of a politics of liberation. Thus, if the positive principles of the first part are partly summarized by the shibboleths of the French Revolution, namely, equality, fraternity, and liberty, then the negative principles—that is, the principles of political critique, or critical politics— are alterity, solidarity, and liberation. If the former begins with the positive and formal affirmation of the right to life of every political subject in a fraternity and formal liberty that acknowledges those who are already treated as equals, then the latter begins from the negativity of the victims of any given political system: these victims could be those whose lives are made impossible by the ruling political system, or they may be victims because they are excluded from the processes of deliberation that endow representatives with political power, or they may be victims because their claims are ignored as either unrealistic, utopian, or unacceptable.

Twenty Theses on Politics also illustrates a major tenet of Dussel's philosophy, namely that there is no mere universality but rather always a universal claim that is particularly and singly articulated. The abstract is not the most universal, and the concrete is the most universal. This is exhibited in the dialectical arch traced by the theses: that is, from the universal particularity of the last decade of constitutional assemblies in Latin America to the abstract generality of the process of delegation of political power. This work, thus, is not simply a manifesto of a politics of life and for life, but also a manifesto that proclaims and articulates the lessons of the Latin American Left from the last three decades—since the path of military revolution was defeated on the fields of military confrontation by the superior military forces of the United States. To the force of weapons, the Left that matured through the defeats of the 1980s and 1990s has now learned to juxtapose the force of democratic elections and constitutional assemblies. To the Clausewitzian slogan that war is the continuation of politics by other means—which entailed that politics is the continuation of war by other means (as Michel Foucault argued), both formulations thus presupposing and entailing the violence against and obliteration of the opponent—a new slogan is herein proclaimed: politics is the continuation of life through the means of deliberation and delegation whose aim is the very preservation of the opponent. This politics is a biopolitics—a politics not only of the preservation, enhancement, and continuation of the life of the political community but also of its very condition of material reproduction: the planet earth, the cultural communities, and the traditions within which naked life is transformed in political life.

This book, then, is both a summary and an introduction to what will surely become Enrique Dussel's magnum opus. While the world is hurled into the whirlwind of economic chaos, political ineptitude, and impending ecological disaster by the forces of neoliberalism with their cynical and sinister theodicies of progress, the dispossessed masses of the world clamor for a planetary politics. Dussel's book seeks to give voice to this clamoring by positing once again what was one of the greatest discoveries of early humans—namely that the political is posited by a communal will in order to grant a will to live rational efficacy. Against the gospel of market theologies with their necrophilic idols, Dussel affirms the secularism of the people's determination of their will to live through the noble vocation of the political. Martin Luther's theses were nailed to the gates of the church; Marx's on the gates of dispossessing bourgeois affluence; Dussel's are to be nailed on the walls of the brutal and seemingly unassailable prisons, military bases, banks and board rooms of the IMF, World Bank, and the Pentagon.

These twenty theses on politics are primarily aimed toward young people—
that is, toward those who need to understand that the *noble vocation of politics* is
a thrilling patriotic and collective task.[1] It is true that political activity has
become largely corrupted, especially in postcolonial countries, because our
elites have been governing for five hundred years in the interests of the dominant metropolis of the time (Spain, Portugal, France, England, and today the
United States). There is little press or prestige to be gained by taking into
account those at the bottom: the national political community, the poor,
oppressed, and excluded *people* (see thesis 11).

Recently, Latin America has seen a sort of "political spring," which has been
developing since the birth of many new social movements—the Mothers of the
Plaza de Mayo, the Argentinean *piqueteros*, the movements by the landless and
by the coca farmers, the indigenous movements in Ecuador, Bolivia, Guatemala, and elsewhere—that have come together at the World Social Forum in
Porto Alegre. These movements have coincided with the unexpected elections
of Nestor Kirchner, Tabaré Vásquez, Luiz Inácio Lula da Silva, Hugo Chávez,
Evo Morales, the perennial and proverbial figure of Fidel Castro, and the
symbolic figure of Sub Marcos. These movements and events represent signs
of hope, in the face of which we must begin to create a new theory—a coherent
interpretation of the profound transformation that our *people* are experiencing.

This *new theory* cannot merely respond to the presuppositions of the past five hundred years of capitalist and colonialist Modernity. It cannot set out from bourgeois postulates or from those of *"real"* socialism (with its impossible perfect planning, its squared circle of democratic centralism, its ecological irresponsibility, its bureaucratized cadres, its dogmatic vanguardist theory and strategy, and so on). What is coming is a *new transmodern civilization*, which will be as a result *transcapitalist* and *beyond liberalism* and *real socialism*.

The "Left"—that position occupied by progressive groups in one of the assemblies of the French Revolution—requires a complete ethical, theoretical, and practical renewal. The Left has either governed through its Central Committees or has been in the opposition. Transitioning to the democratic political responsibility of exercising *obediential* power is not an easy task: it is intrinsically participatory and without vanguardism in having learned from the *people* to respect its millennial culture—the mythical narratives within which it has developed its own critical thought and the institutions that must be integrated into this new project.

The twenty-first century demands great creativity. Even socialism, if it still has any meaning, needs to take the form of the "cultural revolution" suggested by Evo Morales (a revolution that has nothing to do with the events in China in 1966). Now is the time of the *people*, of the originary and the excluded. Politics consists of having "the ear of the disciple every morning," so that those who "command, command by obeying." The delegated exercise of *obediential* power (see thesis 4) is a vocation to which the youth is summoned, without personalistic clans, without currents that pursue their own corrupt interests that become corrupted through fighting for the interests of a group rather than that of the whole (whether it be the party, the *people*, the fatherland, or humanity).

The twenty theses in this book, situated at first on an abstract level, become progressively more concrete as they develop. Hence, theses 1 through 10 are the simplest, the most abstract, and the most fundamental, thereby providing the basis upon which the rest of the work is constructed. As Marx suggested, it is necessary to ascend from the abstract to the concrete. Accordingly, theses 11 to 20 are more complex and concrete, since they include the contradiction of the *people* speaking up and taking center stage, thereby entering into action collectively. In the future, new theses should situate these levels with an even greater degree of complexity and concreteness, taking into account the integration of the subjects of colonialism, postcolonialism, metropole, and Empire, and the struggle for liberation from these international forces. There still remains room for other theses, in which all levels of domination and alignment would enter into play on the highest level of complexity, and in which normative principles would confront one another, forcing us to choose one over another (within a situation of inevitable uncertainty). And this is because the *people* do not act as a pure subject, but rather operate through contradictory blocs that frequently throughout history betray their most fundamental demands. How else could entire nations elect Hitler, G. W. Bush, or governments like those of Menem and Fujimori?[2]

ENRIQUE DUSSEL

near Anenecuilco, Morelos,

24 March 2006

INTRODUCTION

[1.01] In order to understand the political (as a concept) and politics (as an activity) it is necessary to spend some time analyzing their essential moments. In general, both the citizen and the politician (by profession or vocation) have failed to meditate sufficiently on the meaning of their function and their political responsibility. In part 1 of this book I examine the diverse moments of the political, its levels and spheres, and especially—in this time of corruption—I address the question of normative political principles. Once I have set forth the minimal moments of politics on an abstract level, I will then be able to ascend to a more concrete, conflictive, and critical level (which will be the subject of part 2).

1 CORRUPTION AND THE POLITICAL FIELD: THE PUBLIC AND THE PRIVATE

[1.1] THE CORRUPTION OF POLITICS

[1.1.1] In order to clear the positive field it is necessary first to enter into the debate regarding what the political "is not." The political is not exclusively any of its components, but rather it is all of these together. A house is not only a door, nor is it only a wall or a roof. To say that politics is one of its isolated components is a reductive fallacy. We need to know how to describe it as a totality. When considered as a totality we can see that there are bad houses, houses that do not allow one to live well, which are too small, which are useless, etc. The same goes for the political.

[1.1.2] The political as such is *corrupted* as a totality when its essential function is distorted or destroyed at its origin. In anticipating what I will explain later [» 5],[1] I begin my reflection on the meaning of the political by first taking a detour—a detour that leads all political actions and institutions completely astray.

[1.1.3] This *originary corruption* of the political, which I will call the *fetishism of power*, consists of the moment in which the political actor (the members of the political community, whether citizens or representatives) believes that power affirms his or her subjectivity or the institution in which he or she functions— as a "functionary," whether it be as president, representative, judge, governor, soldier, police officer [» 7–8]—as the *center* or *source* of political power. This is how, for example, the State comes to be affirmed as the sovereign and as the power of last resort, and this represents the fetishism of the power of the State and the *corruption* of all those who seek to exercise State power defined in this way. If the members of a government, for example, believe that they exercise power through self-referential authority—that is, with reference to themselves—then their power has become *corrupted*.

[1.1.4] Why? Because all exercises of power through any institution (from that of the president to the police) or through any political function (when, for example, citizens meet in open town councils or elect a representative) have as their primary and ultimate reference point the *power of the political community* [» 3–4] (or of the *people* in the strict sense [» 11]). Failing to refer to this power, isolating oneself from it, or cutting the link between the *delegated* exercise of the determinate power of each political institution (*arrow a* in figure 2) and the political power of the community (or the *people*) (*arrow b*) results in the absolutization, the fetishization, and the *corruption* of the power of the representative fulfilling that function.

[1.1.5] This *corruption*, moreover, is double: it corrupts the governors who believe themselves to be the sovereign center of power, and it corrupts the political community that allows itself (consents) to become *servile* rather than be an *actor* in the construction of the political (actions [» 6], institutions [» 7–8], principles [» 9–10]). The *Corrupted* representative can use fetishized power for the pleasure of exercising his or her will as ostentatious vainglory, as despotic high-handedness, as sadism toward his or her enemies or toward the improper appropriation of goods and wealth. It does not matter what apparent benefits are granted to the corrupt governor, as what is worst is not wrongly acquired goods but rather the *diversion* of his or her attention as a representative: from serving the community through the *obediential* exercise of power, the corrupt leader becomes the scourge of the *people*, their "bloodsucker," their parasite, their moment of weakness, and even their death as a political community. Any struggle for one's own interests—whether it be that of an individual (a dictator), a class (e.g., the bourgeoisie), an elite (e.g., Creoles), or a "tribe" (the heirs of old political compromises)—represents the *corruption* of politics.

[1.2.1] Everything that we call *political* (whether it be actions, institutions, principles, etc.) has as its particular space what I will call the *political field*. Every practical activity (events that are family related, economic, sporting, etc.) also has its respective *field* within which the actions, systems, and institutions appropriate to each of these activities are carried out.

[1.2.2] I will use the concept of a *field* approximately as it was used by Bourdieu.[2] This category allows us to situate the various possible levels or spheres of political actions and institutions, in which the subject operates as the *actor* with respect to a given function or as the participant in multiple practical horizons within which numerous *systems* and *subsystems* are structured (to use the terminology of Luhmann).[3] These *fields* are carved out from the totality of the "world of everyday life."[4] Of most interest here are the practical *fields*.

[1.2.3] The subject, then, becomes present in these *fields* through functionally situating himself or herself in them in various ways. In figure 1 the *subject* is the *S* and appears in *fields* A, B, C, D, and N, which represent the family, local or neighborhood life, urban life, or social layers, for example economic, athletic, intellectual, political, artistic, philosophical modes of existence, and so on indefinitely. The *everyday world* is not the sum of all of these *fields*, nor are the fields the sum of their component *systems*. Rather, the first of these (world, field) comprise and extend beyond the second (fields or systems), as *reality* always exceeds all possible *worlds*, *fields*, or *systems*. This is because, in the end, all three modes are opened and constituted as dimensions of intersubjectivity and also because subjects are always already immersed in intersubjective *networks*—that is, in multiple functional relationships in which they play the position of irreplaceable, living, material *nodes*.[5] There are no fields or systems without subjects (although one could consider a system analytically and abstractly as though it lacked a subject).

[1.2.4] The entire *political field* is traversed by forces, by singular subjects in possession of will and a certain degree of power, and these wills are in turn structured within specific universes. As a result, this *field* is not a mere aggre-

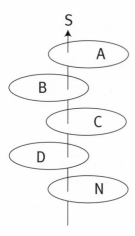

Figure 1. THE SUBJECT (S) ACTS IN VARIOUS FIELDS
Notes: A, B, C, D, N are diverse practical fields (familial, economic, athletic, political, etc.). The subject (S) cuts across these fields, fulfilling differentiated functions in each.

gate of individuals but rather one of intersubjective subjects, always already related through structures of power or institutions of varying permanence. Every subject—as an *actor*—is an *agent* defined in relation to others.

[1.2.5] The *world* of each subject—that is, our world—is composed of multiple *fields*, and each *field*, in turn, can intersect with others, as well as with various *systems*. Subjects *know* how to behave in all of these *fields* and *systems*, as each has cerebral maps that have provided a long apprenticeship in how to *move about* in these *fields* without committing practical *mistakes*—notably, mistakes that *make no sense* within the hermeneutic horizon presupposed by each *field*.

[1.2.6] Each *field* has interest groups, hierarchies, and ways of maneuvering, with respective symbolic, imaginary, and explanatory expressions. One could create, then, a *topography* or *map* of the location of these diverse forces, with respect to which the subject knows how *to act* (see table 1). But this field is not merely a text to be read (as Ricoeur would argue), nor is it a symbol to be decoded or an imaginary to be interpreted, since there equally exist set actions with specific purposes, which are then repeated in institutions and structured through consensus, alliances, and enmities. These fields, then, are practical structures of the power of will as well as narratives to be understood through intersubjective practical reason.

[1.2.7] Fields are those political *spaces* characterized by cooperation, coincidence, and conflict. They are not, accordingly, passive structures (as in struc-

Table 1. SCOPE OF THE CATEGORIES

EXISTENTIAL WORLD	>	POLITICAL FIELD	>	SYSTEMS AND INSTITUTIONS	>	STRATEGIC ACTION
Ontological power		Logic of power		Permanent feasibility. Logic of entropy (Level B)		Contingent feasibility. Logic of contingency (Level A)

Notes: There exist many fields *within a* world. *Similarly, there are many* systems *and institutions within a* field, *and in this book a* system *can also include many* institutions. *Semantically, a* system *is broader than an* institution, *and I will speak, for example, of a* system *of* institutions (e.g., the State). *An* institution *can be a microsystem or a subsystem. At times, however, I use "institutionalization" and "systematization" interchangeably (in which case system and institution would be semantically indistinct). In my terminology "Level C" would be the "implicit principles" [»9–10] that operate on "Level A" and "B" [»6–8].*

turalism) but rather are spheres of interaction that can be not only distinguished from mechanical Cartesian, Newtonian, or Einsteinian logics but also compared to the thermodynamic logic of complexity theory with its bifurcated (or multifurcated) and nonlinear social and political cause-and-effect relations.

[1.2.8] Every *field* is delimited. What falls *outside* the field is beyond its responsibility, and what falls *inside* the field is that which is defined as a component according to the rules that structure those practices permitted within the field. Its *limits* define the surface that determines the sphere of the normative fulfillment of its content, thus differentiating the possible from the impossible.[6] As Karl von Clausewitz states: "We are obliged to say that the *political* object of war is really situated *outside* the sphere of war."[7] Therefore, despite the fact that the fields of politics and war are distinct, the actor can cross from one to the other in an instant.

[1.2.9] Every *field* consists of various *systems*. The political field can be institutionalized through a liberal *system*, a *system* of "real" socialism, or a *system* of increasing participation (as is being attempted in the Bolivarian revolution in Venezuela and in the process led by Evo Morales in Bolivia). Just as *fields* intersect (the *economic* field can intersect with the *political* field), so too do the *systems* present in each field intersect with one another (the *capitalist* system can intersect with the *liberal* system or with a system of postcolonial elites educated in political dependency). The bourgeoisie in the English revolution in the seventeenth century created a parliamentary political *system* that allowed the capitalist economic *system* to carry out the Industrial Revolution (a technological *system* materially subsumed within the capitalist *system*). As we can see, these distinctions are much more appropriate than Althusser's "instance," which is the standard[8] Marxist interpretation.

[1.3] THE PRIVATE AND THE PUBLIC

[1.3.1] The distinction between *private* and *public*[9] refers to various positions or modes of exercising intersubjectivity. Intersubjectivity is the context for existence and meaning where the objectivity of actions and institutions develops. It also contains an a priori mode of *subjectivity* (since there always exists a prior constitutive moment, or a Husserlian passive genesis). For example, to the child, monogamous marriage is an *objective* social institution (*confronting* consciousness as an object) while being simultaneously *below* and *prior*—constituting that very same child's subjectivity through its mother and father. Democracy is an *objective* political institution, which at the same time develops a subjective tolerance in the citizenry from childhood, thereby taking on a purportedly *subjective* character. In other words, all subjectivity is always intersubjective.

[1.3.2] I will deem *private* the operation of the subject in an intersubjective position such that he or she comes to be protected from the presence, from the gaze, and from being attacked by the other members of the multiple intersubjective systems of which he or she forms a part. This sort of practice is external to the *political field*. In a private relation there are always participants (at least two), whose interactions remain private: these are participants in the sphere of those who are the "closest" to us, of "our own," of "relatives." This is why—on the systemic-institutional level—one frequently speaks of the family or of those "within" the walls of the home; namely, the walls that separate us from the "foreign," the "beyond," and the "outside," and from the "elements" and those "dangerous" things that in primitive times terrorized human beings.

[1.3.3] The public sphere, on the other hand, is the *mode* that the subject adopts as an intersubjective position in a "field *with others*," a mode that allows the subject to operate as an "actor" whose "roles" or actions are "represented" *before the gaze of all other actors*. These roles are in turn defined with reference to the foundational story or narrative—the whole *libretto*—of a given political system. To "enter" the public sphere is to "leave" the private sphere, a privacy in which the theatrical set no longer exists and in which one ceases to be an actor and ceases role playing (although roles do exist, in some sense, in the private sphere). There are, then, "limits," "lines," and thresholds, which are continually being crossed and surpassed, either in fulfillment or in transgression of the rules. The public is the sphere of the *ostensible*, and as such the most public place imaginable is that of the representative political assembly, seen and observed responsibly by the represented, who rightfully judge whether or not their interests are correctly represented. Since the time of the Greek "Agora" or the "Great Council" of Venice, politics has been synonymous with "the public."

[1.3.4] That which is done by the politician (*qua* politician) in the obscurity of the nonpublic—but which videos can occasionally make public *for all to see*[10]—is corruption, insofar as it conceals from the represented, from the community, acts that would be unjustifiable in the public light. "Public opinion," on the other hand, is the means by which the political public sphere is nourished.

[2.01] THE PREVAILING POLITICAL ORDER

In part 1 of this book I seek to describe the architectonic moments—the minimum necessary and sufficient conditions—of all possible political orders. Everything I describe here will serve as a foundation that I then *deconstruct* in part 2 [» 11–20]. Do not, therefore, think of me as being merely a conservative, passive, or nonconflictive thinker. The task at hand is to gain consciousness of the different levels and spheres of political architectonics, which are to be then deployed in the political field through a radical notion of political power [» 2–4].

2 THE POLITICAL POWER OF THE COMMUNITY AS *POTENTIA*

[2.1] THE "WILL-TO-LIVE"

[2.1.1] The human being is a living being.[11] All living beings are herd animals, and the human being is a collective being by origin. Since human communities have always been threatened by their vulnerability to death and to extinction, such communities maintain an instinctive desire to remain alive. This *desire-to-live* of human beings in a community can be called a *will*. The *will-to-live* is the originary tendency of all human beings, and I offer this notion as a corrective to Schopenhauer's tragic formulation and the dominating tendency of the "will-to-power" of Nietzsche or Heidegger.

[2.1.2] In Eurocentric Modernity—since the invasion and subsequent conquest of America in 1492—political thought has generally defined *power* as *domination*, a definition that is already present in Machiavelli, Hobbes, and many other classic writers, including Bakunin, Trotsky, Lenin, and Weber, each of whom, however, makes important conceptual distinctions. To the contrary, contemporary social movements require from the outset a *positive* understanding of political power, which nevertheless bears in mind that this power is frequently *fetishized*, corrupted, and denaturalized as *domination*. The "will-to-live" is that positive essence—that content as a force and as a capacity to move, to restrain, and to promote. At its most basic level, this *will* drives us to avoid death, to postpone it, and to remain within human life.

[2.1.3] Toward this end, the living being needs to grasp or to invent the means of survival to satisfy its needs. Such needs are negativities—hunger is the *lack of food*, thirst is the *lack of drink*, cold is the *lack of heat*, ignorance is the *lack of cultural knowledge*, etc.—which must be negated by the existence of basic goods (nourishment *negates* hunger: negation of the prior negation is an affirmation of human life).

[2.1.4] *To-be-able* to take hold of and use such goods to guarantee the means for survival is already *power*.[12] One who *is-not-able* lacks the capacity or faculty *to-be-able* to reproduce or improve her or his life through the fulfillment of the necessary mediations. A slave does not have *power*, in the sense that slaves *are-not-able*, through their own will—as they are neither free nor autonomous—to carry out actions or institutional functions in their own name and for their own good.

[2.1.5] In this sense, in terms of the *content* and *motivation* of power, the "will-to-live" of the members of a community, or of the *people*, is already the fundamental *material* determination of the definition of political power. That is, politics is an activity that organizes and promotes the production, reproduction, and enhancement of the lives of the members of that community. As such, politics could also be referred to as the "general will," notably in its most radical and precise sense as offered by Rousseau.

[2.2] "RATIONAL CONSENSUS"

[2.2.1] But the *wills* of each of the members of the community could also be directed toward the acquisition of their multiple and opposing private interests, and in this way the *potency* or strength of the will of the individual can annul that of others, thereby resulting in *impotence*, or a lack of power. On the other hand, if these wills were able to *join together* their objectives, their purposes, and their strategic ends, then they would achieve—by organically combining strength in a "common-will-to-live"—a higher degree of power-as-potential (*potentia*).

[2.2.2] The possibility of uniting the blind force of will is the proper function of practical-discursive reason. The community, as linguistic and communicative, is one in which its members can provide reasons to other members in order to arrive at agreements. Through the use of a wide range of arguments that represent public rhetorical expressions in reference to the community of wills (e.g., mythical stories, artistic expressions like theater, or even the most abstract scientific formulations), *consensus* can be reached provided that citizens participate symmetrically. Such consensuses—which are occasionally unintentional but accepted by tradition, and as such are no less valid—result in a convergence of wills toward a common good, and this is what we can properly term "political power."

[2.2.3] This *consensus*—or *consensus populi* as Bartolomé de las Casas called it around 1546 in defending the indigenous Peruvians from the Spanish *encomenderos*[13]—cannot be the result of an act of domination or *violence*, in which individual wills are forced to negate their own "desire-to-live" in favor of the "sovereign-desire-to-live" (of the King), as was proposed by Hobbes. In this case, political power finds itself considerably weakened since it is based on a single active, creative will—that of the only actor (the King as State, as despotic Leviathan)—with the remaining citizens having to deny their own wills. Without the foundation of the resolute will of the citizenry—of the political community, the *people*—those in power are themselves weakened, as though they had taken up the artist's brush without the ladder needed to paint. Consensus must be an agreement by *all participants*—as free, autonomous, rational subjects with equal capacity for rhetorical intervention—so that the *solidity of the union of wills* might be sufficiently strong to resist attacks and to create institutions that provide permanence and governability.

[2.2.4] Such consensus is therefore a "communicative power" much like that described by Arendt. The more the individual members of the life-community participate, and the more individual and common demands are satisfied, the more the power of the community—the *power of the people*—becomes through reasoned belief a protective wall and a productive and innovative motor for that community.

[2.2.5] Liberalism affirms the priority of this *formal* moment of the autonomy and liberty of citizens (since Locke), and right-wing politics affirms the primacy of the will, of a more or less irrationalist vitalism (as in the case of Schmitt). What we need to do is to connect both determinations as mutually constitutive and as lacking any determination in the final instance.

[2.3] THE FEASIBILITY OF POWER

[2.3.1] But the consensually united will of the members of the community does not constitute an exhaustive description of *political power*. We still need to discuss one additional element.

[2.3.2] In order to possess the *faculty* for power, the community needs to be able to use mediations—technical-instrumental or strategic—that allow for the empirical exercise of this will-to-live through common (or popular) consensus. If a political community, for example, is attacked by another such community, it needs to be able to resist the attack with military instruments and strategy. If a community suffers famine, it must be able to develop sufficient agricultural systems in order to provide sustenance for the population (as demanded by Aristotle in his *Politics*). If there is little memory of cultural traditions, then the community needs to be able to promote educational, artistic, and historical research programs so that the community, the *people*, might recover a consciousness of its cultural identity—a moment that is equally necessary for the unity of wills as power (and one that represents a central *material* subsphere for politics, as I will show [» 7]).

[2.3.3] *Strategic feasibility* is therefore the third constitutive determination of *political* power, and it can be understood as the potential for using instrumental reason to empirically accomplish the objectives of human life and its historical advancement, within the developed system and the (micro-social or macro-political) institutions that in turn make the other two spheres possible.

[2.3.4] Political power cannot be *taken*, as in the statement "We will attempt to make a revolution through *taking State power!*" Power is *held*, always and only, by the political community—the *people*. The community *always* has this power, whether it be weakened, threatened, or intimidated such that it cannot be expressed. Those who possess pure force—violence, the exercise of openly despotic or ostensibly legitimate domination (as in Weber's description of power)—have only a fetishized, denatured, and spurious power [» 5], which despite being called "power" consists instead of a violence that is destructive of the political itself. Totalitarianism is the exercise of power through nonpolitical, police, or quasi-military means, which cannot awaken in the citizenry that strong consensual union of wills, motivated by free reasoning and discussion, that properly constitutes *political* power.

[2.3.5] I will therefore use the term *potentia* to refer to the power that is a faculty or capacity inherent in the *people* as the final instance of sovereignty, authority, governability, and the political. This power as *potentia*—which spreads like a network over the entire political field, and within which every political actor is a node (to use a category proposed by Castells)—develops on various levels and in various spheres, thereby constituting the foundation and essence of *all that is political*. One might even say that the political is the *development* of political power in all its moments.

INSTITUTIONAL POWER AS *POTESTAS*

3

[3.1] POWER AS *POTESTAS*

[3.1.1] Power is a *faculty* or a *capacity* that one *has* or does not *have*, but to speak precisely, power is never *taken*. What can be assaulted, taken, and dominated are the instruments or institutions that mediate the exercise of power. It is in this sense that one speaks of the "taking of the Bastille"—a prison building that represented the juridical-punitive institutions of the absolutist monarchical State.

[3.1.2] On the other hand, the primary and ultimate collective subject of power, which is as a result sovereign and possesses its own fundamental authority, is always the political community, or the *people*. There is no other subject of power except the community. None!

[3.1.3] *Potentia* [» 2], then, is our starting point, but on its own this power of the community—while representing the ultimate foundation of *all* power—still lacks real, objective, empirical existence. The merely feasible consensual will of the community remains initially *indeterminate* and *in-itself*, that is, it lacks roots, a main stem, branches, and fruit. It could have them, but as yet it does not. The seed is a tree *in-itself*, prior to having manifested itself, realized itself, grown, and appeared in the light of day. In the same sense, power as *potentia* (in its double sense as strength and as future possibility)—while serving as the foundation of all political power—if not actualized (through political action involving power) or institutionalized (through all those political mediations

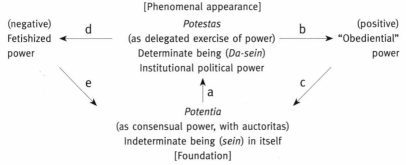

Figure 2. FROM *POTENTIA* TO *POTESTAS*

Notes: Arrow a *represents the originary (ontological) disjunction or split within the primary power (po-tentia) of the political community, which gives rise to the delegation of the exercise of power through institutions and representatives (potestas) ("those who command"). Hegel would have called this dis-tancing the* Diremtion, *the* Entzweiung, *or the* Explicatio *of political power. Originary power (potentia) as such is indeterminate (still not-anything), and is accordingly without any "lack" but also without real or empirical existence. The simple step toward the institutionalization or organization of some hetero-geneous function of one member with respect to another already produces a "determination" ("being there," or* Da-sein*) and inaugurates the possibility of real existence but also at the same time the pos-sibility of the representative distancing himself or herself from the represented, of the institution from the institutionalized, of the* delegated *exercise of power (potestas), which is no longer simply the same con-sensual power "from below" (potentia). Arrow b represents the* positive *exercise of power as a reinforce-ment of potentia. Arrow c represents those who "command obeying" (obediential power). ["Command obeying" is an indigenous phrase popularized by the Zapatista rebellion in Chiapas, Mexico.—Trans.] Arrow d shows the fetishization of potestas (in which institutional power affirms itself as the sovereign origin of power, over and against potentia). Arrow e represents power exercised as domination or a weakening of potentia, in which those in power "rule by command." Arrows a-b-c represent the circula-tion of power as regeneration. Arrows a-d-e represent the corrupt cycle of power.*

required to fulfill the functions of the political), remains merely potential, like a nonexistent possibility.

[3.1.4] If *potentia* is power *in-itself*, then *potestas* is power *outside-itself* (but not necessarily *for-itself*, as we will see). We have illustrated this originary ontologi-cal scission with *arrow a* on figure 2. The process of passing from a fundamen-tal moment (*potentia*) to its constitution as an organized power (*potestas*) begins when the political community affirms itself as an instituting power (but not yet instituted, as Castoriadis suggests), thereby deciding to heterogeneously organize its functions in order to accomplish diverse ends. In the primitive clan there could have been a certain degree of originary indifferentiation (but even then this was not complete): everyone could fulfill all of the functions, because these did not require too much technical experience and because there was little development. In the face of the political complexity of the Neolithic period, however, the appearance of cities required a massive number of occupations and professions, and as a result politics gave rise to multiple institutions (that is, power as *potestas* appeared).

[3.1.5] The necessary institutionalization of the power of the community, of the *people*, constitutes what we term *potestas*. The institutionalized community is one that, having created the mediations that make possible the exercise of *potestas*, splits off from the merely undifferentiated community. This is a scission between *potentia* and *potestas*, in other words, between the power of the political community as central, original, and fundamental (the hidden ontological level) and the heterogeneous differentiation of functions through institutions that allow power to become real, empirical, and feasible, which allow it to appear (as a phenomenon) in the political field. This split—with regard to which we agree with Spinoza and Negri, but simultaneously move beyond them—is necessary, and it marks the pristine appearance of politics while representing at the same time the supreme danger to politics and the origin of all injustice and domination. It is thanks to this scission that all political service becomes possible, but it is here that all corruption and oppression also begins its uncontrollable course. *Being* (*sein*) becomes *being-that* (*Dasein*)—a thing—and as a result both justice and its opposite enter into history. The anarchist dreams of the lost paradise of *potentia*, of undifferentiated power in-itself (in which injustice is impossible), and the conservative adores the fixed and controlled power of *potestas* (and accordingly exercises institutional power as domination). Politics will be the long history of the proper or corrupted use of *potestas*. The *noble vocation of politics* is a possibility that opens up only with this primary scission (indicated with the move from *arrow a* toward *arrow b* in figure 2). The other possibility is the idolatrous and corrupt vocation of power as self-referential *potestas*, which always becomes the scourge of the *people* (in the process that begins with *arrow d* and culminates in *arrow e*).

[3.2.1] Power as potential always and only belongs to the political community, the *people*. It becomes *real* thanks to institutionalization (*potestas*), which mediates strategic action [» 6] and which, as such, represents the agential moment but not the stabilizing historical outcome. That is, the *exercise of power* is always a moment of *potestas*, or of institutionally fixed functions [» 7], since strategic political action—which takes the form, in the initial case of a *constituent* power (*potentia* as an *instituting* power in the creation of a constitution), of all that leads up to the convocation of the representatives for the constituent assembly —is in some way framed by the natural democratic institution (as Francisco Suárez describes it).[14] This is because, in effect, when a community agrees to create a government this decision must be made collectively, and to do so is already a democratic act akin to the natural discursive symmetry of *potentia* in the first institutional act. Whether this *potestas* is institutionalized as a monarchical or republican system, or as an oligarchic or democratic republic, etc., can be decided later, and once *potestas* is sufficiently institutionalized, the normal exercise of delegated power in the hands of the representatives can begin.

[3.2.2] But in fact, any exercise of power is institutional, because the power of the community as *potentia* in-itself is not an initial empirical moment in time but rather a foundational moment that always remains in force *beneath* institutions and actions (that is, beneath *potestas*). When one speaks, then, of the "exercise of power" it means that this power is actualized as one of its institutional possibilities, and like all mediation it is heterogeneously determined. The exercise of electoral power as a citizen is not the same as the exercise of presidential power as the head of government. Both, however, are an *exercise* or an actualization—that is, the phenomenal appearance of an action in the political field or an institution fulfilling a function through its operator. Institutional exercise, then, is not power as *potentia*. The community possesses the originary and ontological faculty of power, but any actualization of that power is institutional and thereby *delegated*. The slogan "All power to the soviets!" draws us toward the direct and fully participative democracy of the community in possession of *potentia*. Regardless, while the soviets already represented a certain minimal degree of institutionalization, they lacked some essential institutional levels—the soviets were a *potentia* that did not want to become alienated as *potestas*—and as a result the effort failed categorically. With the birth of "real" or "actually existing" socialism in the Soviet Union in 1921—in which the "soviets" remained in name only—*potestas* was excessively consolidated and passed from a situation of quasi-anarchism (in which *potentia* is always idealized) to a totalitarian organization of *potestas*. Neither the first position (of lack) nor the second (of excess) is adequate.

[3.2.3] That is, the community cannot permanently behave as a substantive and unanimous collective actor through direct democracy. This is the ideal moment of the postulate, but it remains empirically impossible [» 15 and 19] since the community acts in a differentiated manner through each of its members. During the Paleolithic hunt, one member of the party would give the signal to begin the hunt, others frightened the prey, others brandished arms in appropriate places, others specialized in the use of traps, and still others distributed the catch proportionally among the hunters. This functional differentiation allowed them to achieve higher and more complex objectives, and the same can be said of the *delegated* exercise of political power.

[3.2.4] *Delegation* implies that one is to act in the name of all (universality) through a differentiated function (particularity) undertaken through individual attention (singularity). The *singular* (private) exercise of an action is that which is carried out in one's own name. The *delegated* (public) exercise of an action is carried out as a function of the whole, and the foundation of this exercise is the power of the community (as *potentia*). Those who exercise power in this way do so through others (with regard to origin), as mediation (with regard to content), and for the other (with regard to purpose: *arrow c* in figure 2).

[3.3] *POTESTAS* AS OBJECTIFICATION, ALIENATION

[3.3.1] In the economic field, the living labor of the worker is objectified in the value of the product. This objectification—through which, by being transformed into *another* thing, the labor becomes "alienated"—can be understood as similar to the coagulation of blood, since blood is the symbol of life in Semitic thought. Similarly, in the political field the power of the *people* (*potentia*) is objectified and alienated in the *system* of political institutions produced historically throughout the millennia for the exercise of that power (as *potestas*).

[3.3.2] To speak of the objectification of a collective subjectivity like that of the political community necessarily implies a certain degree of estrangement, a loss of immediate identity, and a move toward mediated differentiation. Mediation is necessary since the reproduction of life is impossible without institutions and systems (e.g., agriculture and shepherding) since no legitimacy can be accepted without intersubjective agreements, and since political power is impossible without these prerequisites. But at the same time, this mediation remains opaque and nontransparent—as simultaneously necessary and ambiguous as representation and indeed all institutions [» 7].

[3.3.3] Like all mediation, *potestas* (as the sum of institutions) is therefore ambiguous. Its normative meaning as justice or its cynical use as violent force exist in an originary state in which necessary discipline always represents a certain form of the compulsion of pleasure, and as such could be interpreted as repression. However, by its nature and in the first moments of its creation, the institutions of *potestas* generally respond to some popular demands. Quickly— although this can be a matter of centuries—these institutions show on the one hand signs of fatigue through a process of entropy and erosion, and on the other hand the inevitable fetishization that bureaucracy produces in institutions (*potestas*), turning them toward the survival of a self-referential bureaucracy. When this happens, the mediations invented for the advancement of life and democracy turn instead down the path toward death, repression, and domination. The critical political actor—one who has an attitude of *critical realism*—must embark upon the course that seeks to be the most critical, that of the "Left," which today, beyond being merely opposed to the Right, has ceased to put forth its own concrete political content.

[3.3.4] In this case, alienation as mere objectification becomes the negation of the *delegated* exercise of power, that is, it becomes the fetishized exercise of that power.

OBEDIENTIAL POWER

4

[4.1] POLITICS AS A "PROFESSION" OR A "VOCATION"

[4.1.1] In *Politics as a Vocation*,[15] Max Weber describes how for the subject the political function can be interpreted and lived—existentially and biographically—as a bureaucratic "profession" (in some cases, a very lucrative one) or as a "vocation" motivated by ideals and values with a normative content that inspires the subjectivity of the political actor toward a responsibility to the other, to the *people*. Today, at the beginning of the twenty-first century, politicians—representatives elected for the exercise of institutional power, or *potestas*—represent elitist groups that have become progressively corrupted, notably in light of the enormous erosion of twentieth-century revolutions, the failure of many political movements encouraged by grand ideals, and the economic crisis, and in a context marked by the increasing difficulty for young people to find fixed salary positions (due to increasing structural unemployment).

[4.1.2] It is impossible to motivate the young to choose politics—or to reinvigorate those who chose it long ago—through an appeal to outdated virtues or to the abstract values of a decadent aristocratic society. Young people—bombarded by the mediaocracy, by fashion, and by the totality of an everyday world immersed within the horizon of capitalist society, which imposes its superficial and ostentatious ideals through the market—will have a difficult time overcoming the demands to increase their wealth in order to be able to buy and show off these (monetarily) expensive signs of difference (as

Baudrillard would say). It is not impossible, then, to imagine that those who choose the profession of politics might quickly accept the Faustian bargain, and "sell their soul to the devil" of fetishization by using the exercise of power for their own individual or group purposes. This is the birth of politics as a "profession" and political parties as "electoral machines" that impose their bureaucratized candidates to benefit their own party. This is the fetishization of power through the corruption of the subjectivity of the political actor.

[4.1.3] Against this issue we need to struggle for the birth and growth of a new generation of patriots—of young people who decide to create "another politics," as was done by Spartacus, Joan of Arc, Washington, Hidalgo or Bolivar, and even by "Che" Guevara, Fidel Castro, or Evo Morales. None of these figures were political by "profession." They were slaves, shepherds, landowners, priests or intellectuals, doctors, lawyers, and unionists, but through ethical responsibility they came to serve their communities, their *people*, and in many cases they gave their lives for their cause. What more can one offer than one's life? Those who survived demonstrated an incorruptible fidelity to the delegated exercise of power in favor of their *people*: they did not flaunt delegated authority in order to increase their prestige or wealth. Their glory—still greater for having been persecuted by the enemies of the *people* who they liberated—consists of their efforts to be faithful to the end in perseverance to their "vocation."

[4.1.4] "Vocation" (from the Latin verb *vocare*) means "to be called upon" to complete a mission. The one who "calls" is the community, the *people*, and the one who is called feels "summoned" to assume the responsibility of service. All happiness to those who faithfully fulfill their vocation! Cursed be those who betray it, because they will be judged either in their own time or by history! On September 11, 1973, Augusto Pinochet seemed to be an untouchable and demiurgic hero, and the humiliated democratic and popular leaders like Salvador Allende died in his armor-plated hands. In 2006, Pinochet was on trial, not just for being a dictator but for robbing the *people* (also on trial were his wife and children). Who would have suspected this at the time of the coup d'etat, when he was supported by Henry Kissinger and all of the powerful leaders of the West? Carlos Menem and Carlos Salinas de Gortari will enjoy the same luck.

[4.2] POWER AS "OB-EDIENCE"

[4.2.1] Those who lead are representatives who must fulfill a function of *potestas*. They are elected to exercise *in a delegated manner* the power of the community, and they must do so with respect to the demands, claims, and needs of that community. When in examining the events in Chiapas we are taught that "those who command must[16] command by obeying," this is a very precise indication of the service of the political functionary (fulfilling a "function"), who exercises *delegated, obediential* power (*arrow b* in figure 2).

[4.2.2] In this way, we have a categorical circle that remains positive—that is, one that has not yet fallen into the fetishizing corruption of power as domination. The power of the community (*potentia*) gives rise to political institutions (*potestas*) (*arrow a* in figure 2) operating through delegation to elected representatives (*arrow b*) in order to fulfill the demands of the fullest life of the citizenry (material sphere [» 7]), with reference to the demands of the system of legitimacy (formal sphere [» 8]), and within the realm of the strategically feasible. The representative is *attributed* a certain degree of authority—because the center of *auctoritas* is not the government, but rather always in the final instance the political community (although Agamben does not specify this)—in order to better carry out the responsibilities of his or her position in the name of the whole (of the community). Representatives do not act *from themselves* as a final source of sovereignty and authority, but rather as delegates and with regard to their objectives (*arrow c* in figure 2)—that is, in favor of the community, listening to its demands and claims. "To listen to the one before you,"[17] is to say that obedience is the primary subjective position that the representative or governor,[18] or those performing the function of a political institution, must have.

[4.2.3] *Obediential* power would therefore mean the delegated exercise of the power of all authority that fulfills the political justice claim.[19] Put differently, this characterizes the upright political actor who aspires to exercise power in order to have the necessary subjective position to struggle in favor of the empirically possible happiness of a political community, a *people*.

[4.2.4] This circle—indicated by *arrows a, b, and c* in figure 2—is a process that produces, reproduces, and enhances the life of the community and each one of its members, fulfilling the requirements of democratic legitimacy within the horizon of a critical realism that grasps instrumental and strategic feasibility while keeping sight of the normative [» 10].

[4.2.5] In this way, we have sought to describe power, in its proper sense, *positively* (and not merely as domination)—namely as the strength and the consensual will that produces actions and gives rise to institutions that support the political community. Each of these institutions—from the micro-institutions of civil society (to which Foucault pays so much attention [» 8.3.3]) to the macro-institutions of political society (so criticized by Bakunin [» 8.3.4])— exercises a certain degree of power, in structures disseminated throughout the political field and within specific systems, such that within each of these the institutions can fulfill this *obediential* character. The political field, in the strictest sense, is not an empty space but rather is like a minefield full of networks and nodes ready to explode over conflicts about unfulfilled demands (bearing in mind that one can never fulfill all such demands perfectly).

[4.3] REPRESENTATION AND "SERVICE"

[4.3.1] The representative—as the name indicates—"represents" the citizen *qua* member of the political community who upon electing the representative thereby constitutes his or herself as the "represented." There is a certain inevitable passivity in this gesture, which also carries with it a certain degree of risk. The risk consists of the fact that while the delegation of originary power— that of the community, *potentia*—is necessary (against the *spontaneism* of certain types of populism and anarchism), and while this delegation must be continuously regenerated through the face-to-face interaction of a community assembly (below the municipal level—i.e., neighborhood assemblies, communes, rank-and-file committees, etc.), there nevertheless remains the risk of fetishization. In other words, representation too can turn inward on itself and become self-affirming as the final instance of power.

[4.3.2] I repeat: Power is "delegated" to someone so that they might "represent" the community, the *people*, on the level of the institutional exercise of power. This is necessary but at the same time ambiguous. It is necessary because direct democracy is impossible in political institutions that involve millions of citizens. But it is ambiguous because the representative can forget that he or she exercises power through delegation, in the name "of another," as one who is "presented" on the institutional level (*potestas*) with reference ("re-") to the power of the community (*potentia*). Representation, then, is obedience.

[4.3.3] In its fullest, original, political sense, representation is the delegation of power for the purpose of being exercised or fulfilled in "service" to the represented, who have elected a representative because neither the advancement of life in the community nor legitimacy nor efficacy are possible without the differentiation of heterogeneous functions. If in the Paleolithic hunt everyone performed the same function (e.g., sounding the alert), then no one would be able to catch anything. Or, if each person merely performed the function that they preferred, the result would be chaos and the hunters would never be able to capture the swift rabbit or the fierce lion. Instead, they would die of hunger. Representation, then, is necessary but ambiguous, but it cannot be eliminated on account of this ambiguity. Rather, it is necessary to define it, to regulate it, and to imbue it with normativity such that it might be useful, efficient, just, and obedient to the community.

[4.3.4] Having said this, and in transition to the next *thesis*, we can now understand that power divides once again. This time, however, the split does not occur between *potentia* (power in-itself) and *potestas* (power as mediation), but rather in an entirely new way.

[4.3.5] In the first place, we have *positively*, *obediential* power ("commanding by obeying") [explained here in *thesis 4*], which we can see described in the following well-known text: "Whoever wants to be first [i.e., an *authority*] must be a *slave*[20] to all"[21] (*arrow b* in figure 2). In this case, the *delegated* exercise of power is carried out through *vocation* and *compromise* with the political community, with the *people*.

[4.3.6] In the second place, we have *negatively fetishized* power [» 5] ("commanding by commanding"), which is condemned with the warning that "those who are regarded as rulers . . . *dominate* the *people* as though they were their bosses, . . . their high officials exercise *authority* over them"[22] (*arrow d* in figure 2). In this case, the self-referential exercise of power is performed for the benefit of the governor and his or her group, "tribe," sector, or bourgeois class, etc. The representative in this case is a *corrupt bureaucrat* who turns his or her back on and oppresses the political community, the *people*.

THE FETISHIZATION OF POWER:
POWER AS DOMINATION

5

[5.1] WHAT IS FETISHISM?

[5.1.1] The strange word "fetishism" comes from Portuguese, in which *fetiço* means "done."[23] In the sense that things "made by the hands of man" are idols, fetishism is similar to idolatry, as both terms refer to the making of "gods" through the imaginative control of the human being. These gods are "made," but then are worshiped as divine, as absolute, and as the origin of all else, and it was for this reason that the young Karl Marx—under the restricted press freedom of the despotic Prussian king—wrote this magnificent text: "*We will do what we like* [says the government]. *Sic volo, sic jubeo, stat pro ratione voluntas.*[24] It is truly the language of a ruler [*Herrschersprache*]. . . . Of course, the province has the right, under prescribed conditions, to create *these gods* for itself,[25] but as soon as they are created, it must, like a fetish worshipper, forget that these *gods are its own handiwork.*[26] . . . We are confronted here with the peculiar spectacle, due perhaps to the nature of the Provincial Assembly,[27] of the province having to fight not so much *through its representatives* as *against them.*"[28]

[5.1.2] This explicitly political text by Marx shows us that fetishism in politics has to do with the absolutization of the "will" of the representative, which ceases to respond, ceases to base itself on and link itself to the "general will" of the political community it represents: "Thus I wish it, thus I order it; the will [of the governor] takes the place of *reason* [as foundational]." The foundational link between *potestas* (the power that must be exercised through *delegation*) and *potentia* (the power of the *people* itself) is broken, and the former is thereby absolutized, claiming itself as a self-reflexive and self-referential foundation.

[5.1.3] Within the economy, Marx explains this *inversion* more broadly, formulating it as the "personification of the thing and a reification of the person,"[29] to which he adds the following: "Living labour is incorporated into capital . . . [and] appears as an *activity belonging to capital*, as soon as the labour process starts. . . . Thus the productive power of social labour, and the specific forms of it, now *present themselves as* productive powers and forms of capital. . . . Here once again we have the inversion of the relation, the expression of which we have already characterized as the *fetishism* of the commodity."[30]

[5.1.4] This *inversion* consists of the fact that "living labor" (or the living, corporeal subjectivity of the worker: the "person") is the basis of all value (and capital is nothing more than "the accumulated valorization of value"), that is, the basis of capital (the "thing"). Now, on the other hand, the thing-like product of living labor (capital) becomes a "person" or a phenomenal subject, and the worker becomes a "thing" (instrument) in the service of the growth of capital. Fetishism is this spectral inversion: the founded, the edifice, appears as the foundation and the foundation as the founded, the edifice. This is the "fetishistic secret of capital," that is, its method of concealment that distorts interpretation and knowledge of reality by inverting it.

[5.1.5] The same occurs in politics, as *potestas* or institutionalized power—which is the *delegated* exercise of the originary power of the community or *people (potentia)*—now affirms itself as the center, as the foundation, as the *being*, as *political power properly speaking*. The "will" of the governor, the representative, the institutions, the State—which Marx expresses correctly as the moment in which "will takes the place of *reason*"[31]—becomes the location of political power on behalf of that same governor. "Those who command, command by commanding," and they command the obedient (as required by Weber). *Potentia* has been de-potentiated and has become a passive mass that receives orders from political power (dominant classes, powerful elites, political institutions, the State, the Leviathan). *Potestas* has been deified, separated from its origin (indicated by *arrow a* in figure 2), and self-referentially turned in upon itself (*arrows a-d-e* illustrate this fetishist movement).

[5.1.6] Once power has become fetishized, the action of the representative, of the governor (whether it be a king, a liberal parliament, a state, etc.), must inevitably be a *coercive* action and thus cannot fulfill the *delegated* exercise of the power of the community. This, as I mentioned, represents the predominant understanding of power from the perspective of colonialist Modernity and Empire since Hobbes. However procedural the elections, and however much institutions like the popular election of representatives appear to have been fulfilled, this is still only the self-referential exercise of despotic authority. Representation itself has become corrupted, and election yields coercion. All of politics has been *inverted*, or fetishized.

[5.2] FETISHIZATION OF POWER

[5.2.1] Fetishism begins with the subjective debasement of the individual representative who has the pleasure, the desire, and the sadistic force of the omnipotent exercise of fetishized power over disciplined and obedient citizens. The nonobedient, in turn, are the object of police repression—the definition of Kant's understanding of politics as the coercive *legality* of the *external* liberal State, which accordingly does not demand the subjective adhesion of morality. It is this that Schmitt rightly shows as the radical destruction of the *content* of politics and that Habermas explains as the lack of a sufficient foundation for *legitimacy*. Such exercise is always domination. This is treated as an Act of God, as by the Roman slave, by the feudal serf, or by the citizen who stoically suffers this despotic exercise of power by cultivating virtues in this life and awaiting deserved happiness in the next (as shown by Kant, a professor in Königsburg, a city that claimed membership in the Hanseatic League).

[5.2.2] When power is defined institutionally, objectively, or systematically *as domination*—in the best of cases claiming to represent the power *of the people*,[32] *by* the *people*,[33] and *for* the *people*[34]—popular demands can never be fulfilled, because power functions as a separate, extrinsic, coercive instance "from above" *acting on* the *people*. This was the case of the "democratic centralism" of the Central Committee of "real" socialism, and equally with liberalism, in which the bourgeoisie—always a minority by definition—gain the majority through deceptive electoral procedures perpetrated on the masses, who remain bewildered by the fetishistic mechanisms of the mediaocracy. In effect, the originary power of the community, the *people* (*potentia*), is expropriated from it and proclaimed to serve it *from without, from above* like an eagle,[35] and also like a Monster, like the Leviathan, leading the *people* to exclaim: "Have all the workers of iniquity no knowledge, who eat up my *people* as they eat bread?" (Psalm 14:4; a passage to which Marx, who was from a family of Jewish rabbis from Trier, often turns).

[5.3] DERIVATIONS OF THE FETISHIZATION OF POWER

[5.3.1] The fetishization of power, as we have seen, consists of a "Will-to-Power" as domination of the *people*, of the majority, of the weakest, of the poor. All other definitions must be rejected as idealistic, insufficiently realistic, moralistic, and ineffective. In this case, politics is the art of exercising power over antagonists who are subjected—at best, hegemonically—to the will of fetishized institutions in favor of some particular members of the community or, in the case of postcolonial countries (like those of Latin America), for the benefit of metropolitan States. This same fetishized power, since it cannot base itself on the strength of the *people*, must support itself through groups that violently subjugate that very same *people* or must rely on metropolitan, imperial powers when the dominant consensus has lost its effectiveness in producing the *obedience* of the masses (that is, when Weberian legitimacy is no longer accepted). Carlos Menem and Carlos Salinas de Gortari were both very highly regarded in the United States and also at the World Bank and at the International Monetary Fund. They behave despotically toward those below and submissively toward those above: they are "viceroys" or provincial governors, but not "kings."

[5.3.2] In order to be able to exercise self-referential power—the fetishization of *potestas*—it is necessary to have previously, and to continue to weaken, the originary political power of the community (*potentia*). *Potestas* destroys *potentia* (*arrow e* in figure 2). That is, it divides the community, it impedes the construction of a consensus "from below," and it sows conflict. As the fetishist adage states, "Divide and conquer." Self-referential power can only triumph if it destroys the originary and normative power of all politics: the power of the political community. This is why dictators—Hitler and Pinochet on one side and Stalin on the other, bearing in mind the differences between the two—repress the citizenry, civil society, the political community, the *people*. Nothing and no one could provide a foundation for anti-democratic action [» 8 and 10]. Fetishized power is essentially anti-democratic, as we will see, because it is self-grounded on its own despotic will.

[5.3.3] Fetishized power expects compensation. In the feudal world, for example, publicly recognized honor was the fruit of the despotic exercise of the power of the feudal lord over the serfs and the cities. Their "Will-to-Power" was satisfied by political and religious power over their domain. In capitalist society, on the other hand, in which capital serves as the supreme value, triumph is measured according to the increasing wealth of the citizens. Wealth is the payment afforded to those who surrender their lives to the profession of politics (as a prominent member of a party or as a representative in congress) when power has become corrupted and fetishized. And while salaries, however high, are never enough for the boundless avarice that gloats over the exercise of limitless power, the accumulation of wealth through illegitimate means quickly presents itself as a possibility. Furthermore, the subjective corruption resulting from the theft of public goods—through illegal enrichment such as the discovery of sixty million dollars in a Swiss bank account on behalf of a nepotistic politician: corruption as robbing the *people* of Mexico—and the will to dominate that such corruption entails surreptitiously slides toward the sexual domination of the subaltern woman. I am speaking here of an unconscious subjective confusion in which the *libido* or pleasure at exercising despotic power over the other, the avarice of accumulating their goods, and the erotic domination of their bodies, all intersect with one another.

[5.3.4] The political bureaucracies of parties become corrupted when they use those mediations necessary for the exercise of power toward their own ends. They cease to be representatives who act through *delegation* and instead become despots who demand that the *people* pay homage to their authority. The *inversion* is repeated. Instead of the *people* being served by the representative they become its servant. The elites, the political class, appear as self-referential, and they no longer respond to the political community.

[5.3.5] The various "currents" existing within the parties (vulgarly called "tribes") fight for their "power quota" so that their preferred candidates might stand for the election of representatives. In short, they fight so that their most capable members might occupy a position in the *system* of the political institutions of the State, thereby guaranteeing them an income. This is proof of corruption, because they have forgotten their responsibility as actors that need to be prepared and to carry out a role, to be representatives in the *delegated* and *obediential* exercise of power with respect to the *potentia* of the *people*. Insofar as they do not care about the honor of their own party or the common good of the community, and insofar as they practice violent, dishonest, crooked, or fraudulent means in order to become bought-and-paid-for representatives, political actors express a profound corruption. The *people* lose confidence in candidates or authorities whose ethical coherence—with regard to their family, their finances, their conduct in the party and in public, etc.—demonstrates clear contradictions. A modern party is not an electoral mechanism but rather a body of public servants with a thoughtful, studied, well-crafted ideology carried out always through public political actions.

[5.3.6] There can be corruption among popular groups. For example, corporatism is the effort to cater to private interests through collaboration with the fetishized power of those who govern; here we might think, for example, of an oil union that seeks profit through favors that harm public well-being in order to prevent the mobilization of workers against the privatization of petroleum. Many seek power from above in order to benefit from the crumbs of its corruption, and in so doing they make possible that very same corruption. Even though all sectors of society might be part of a corporative structure that struggles for its particular interests, the demands of the *people* still would not have been fulfilled in such a situation: there would simply be a multitude of gangs of thieves struggling among themselves without being able to construct even the most minimal agreement deserving of the name of political power "from below," from the *people* as *potentia*. The internal rules of a band of thieves have nothing to do with political normativity.

[5.3.7] Even groups of *people* can become corrupted, as when the population of the Empire maintains its silence or looks the other way in the face of the immolation of innocent *people* like those of Afghanistan, Iraq, or Palestine; or like the German *people*, the immense majority of which "did not find out" about the extermination of Jews in the Holocaust.[36]

STRATEGIC POLITICAL ACTION 6

[6.0.1] Power unfolds over the entire political field, blanketing it with a network of force relations and nodes (each citizen, each representative, and each institution represents one of these "knots"). I would like to propose for the sake of clarity, however, that there are three *levels* within which we can deal with all of the moments that constitute politics (see figure 3). The first *level* (A) is that of strategic action [» 6, 15–16]. The second *level* (B) is that of the institutions [» 7–8, 17–20] that constitute a political order. The third *level* (C), which crosses the other two, represents the implicit normative principles of all prevailing political orders as well as those on the verge of transformation [» 9–10, 13–14]. I will now proceed to indicate the contents of these *three architectonic levels* of politics. Levels B and C will each contain, in turn, three *spheres* [» 7.0]

[6.1] STRATEGIC ACTION

[6.1.1] Political action—to which Machiavelli dedicated his book *Il Principe*—is the *actuality* of the political actor in the political *field*. By this action, the citizen makes himself or herself publicly present in the exercise of some moment of power. This action, moreover, represents par excellence the contingent and the uncertain. For Machiavelli it was *Fortuna* that expressed the unforeseeable

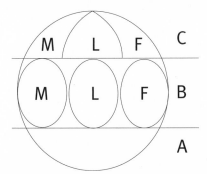

Figure 3. THE THREE *LEVELS* OF THE POLITICAL AND THE THREE *SPHERES* THAT CONSTITUTE
THE INSTITUTIONAL AND NORMATIVE *LEVELS*

Notes: A is the level of strategic action; B is the level of institutions; and C is the level of normative principles. M is the material sphere in B or the material principle in C; L is the sphere of the system of democratic legitimacy in B or the democratic principle in C; and F is the sphere of feasibility in B or the principle of strategic feasibility in C.

character of what occurs in this sphere. *Fortuna* is like a torrential rain capable of destroying everything, and accordingly it is necessary to construct dikes in order to restrain and direct it (what Machiavelli would call *virtù*). The problem to be resolved, then, is to find some logic in action—that is, some way to bring that action to a positive conclusion and to do so in an empirically efficient and *possible* way, since what is logically and ideally possible might very well be *empirically impossible* and thus *beyond* the horizon of the political field, although some may stubbornly attempt it nevertheless.

[6.1.2] Political action is *strategic* and not merely instrumental (as is the case with technical action that transforms nature), since it is directed toward other human subjects that as actors occupy practical spaces, enter into hierarchies, and offer resistance or contribute to the action of others, in a force field that constitutes what we have deemed *power*. Therefore, consensual will provides collective actions with the strength, the unity, and the power necessary to achieve its goals.

[6.1.3] This strategic action requires the faculty of practical reason, which the ancients called *prudence* (*phronesis*). In China, as Sun Tzu explains in his treatise on war, "the capable warrior looks for victory by studying *strategic potential (shi)*. . . . It is the nature of logs and stones that they are inoffensive when on flat ground but dangerous when on a slope. . . . Hence, the *strategic potential (shi)* of a competent army is like that of an avalanche of stones rolling down from the top of the mountain."[37]

[6.1.4] "Strategic potential" is the practical structure that confronts the political actor as a matter of fact. It is the complex conjunctural situation of the strength of all the actor's allies and antagonists that one needs to be able to assess in order to know how to utilize it toward the proposed objectives. It is often most effective to do nothing.

[6.1.5] For Max Weber, political action is in the final instance domination: "'Domination' (*Herrschaft*) is the probability that a command with a given specific content will be obeyed by a given group of persons."[38]

[6.1.6] As I have shown, power is the consensual will of the community or the *people*, which in its first moment demands the obedience of the authority.[39] Weber has inverted the question, making the institution the seat of power as *domination*, which then demands the obedience of society.

[6.1.7] Carl Schmitt, in struggling against the formal and legalistic evacuation that characterizes liberal individualism, proposes that the essence of political action turns on the "friend-enemy" dialectic. He rightly distinguishes between (a) a private "enemy" or rival (*ekhthrós* in Greek), (b) the public "enemy" or antagonist (*hostis* in Latin), and (c) the total "enemy," to whom death is given in war (enemy in the broad sense; *polémos* in Greek). What is determining is that the criterion of difference between "enemy" (b) and "enemy" (c) consists, in short, of a certain *fraternity* (as understood by Derrida)[40] that brings together friends and political antagonists (who are, in the end, all members of the same community or *people*) and separates them from "others" (beyond the national or popular organization). However, again, if we place ourselves on the horizon of humanity—a horizon that Schmitt attempts to deny through his Eurocentric nationalism—there would be a *universal fraternity* like that postulated by Kant, which might someday achieve *perpetual peace*. Such peace would demonstrate that political action is based more upon fraternity, a positive value, than on pure enmity, which while existing needs to be disciplined in order to arrive at a *political* relationship (and indeed the *political* element of the action is precisely that which promotes the friendship of citizens rather than destructive opposition).[41]

[6.2] HEGEMONIC ACTION

[6.2.1] Properly political action is not by nature violent or coercive, because this would destroy the essence of political power and would weaken *potestas* by removing its foundation. But neither can political action attempt to fulfill a perpetually unanimous direct democracy.[42] Such political action is, in the best of cases, "hegemonic"—that is, it is based on the consensus of the determinant majority. *Consensus*—which unites wills and binds power as a joint force—can be achieved, but it cannot do so in a *perfect* manner since perfect agreements would be, again, unanimity. The question, therefore, is how can a political community, a *people*, achieve a sufficient consensus in order to make possible the exercise of power and citizen participation?

[6.2.2] The actions of each social sector, be they of Civil Society or even of the purely social sphere [» 7], refer to particular demands. Feminism struggles for the respect of the rights of women in the face of *masculinist patriarchy*; anti-racist movements make an effort to eliminate discrimination against non-whites; and movements of the elderly are equally mobilized on the basis of their demands, as are marginal and informal workers, the traditional working class, the peasantry, indigenous peoples, ecologists, etc. All of these differential movements within a country—which come together on the global scale at the World Social Forum in Porto Alegre—cannot remain in the pure opposition of contradictory or incommunicable claims.

[6.2.3] A hegemonic demand (or a coherently structured group of demands) is one that manages to unify all claims—or at least those most urgent for everyone—within a broader proposal.[43] Struggles over demands constitute political actions, and if these actions achieve the level of unity [» 11], we can say that they have become hegemonic. This does not mean that there are no antagonistic groups opposing minorities whose claims will need to be dealt with in the future. The fact is that political action needs to be extremely attentive in observing, respecting, and including, if possible, the interests of all groups, sectors, and movements. When an action becomes hegemonic, it begins to mobilize the power of the community or the *people* (as *potentia*), and the actions of representatives flow toward their objective with the support of the strength and motivation of all, or at least the most significant sectors. Hegemonic action is the fully delegated exercise of power (*potestas*), and it relies on consensus, fraternity, and the *people* as the foundation of power. In twentieth-century Latin America, leaders like Vargas in Brazil (1930–1954), Cárdenas in Mexico (1934–1940), Perón in Argentina (1946–1955), and many other leaders deemed "populists" were examples of this type of hegemonic action.[44]

[6.2.4] In accordance with this understanding of hegemony, Hannah Arendt reminds us that "power is always, as we would say, a power *potential* and not an unchangeable, measurable, and reliable entity like force or [physical] strength. While strength is the natural quality of an individual seen in isolation, power springs up between men when they act together and vanishes the moment they disperse."[45]

[6.2.5] Only hegemonic action—which exists between violence and a politically impossible unanimity (the latter of which is, however, technically feasible under totalitarianism)—allows the essence of political power to appear phenomenally in the political field. Other types of action represent its negation.

[6.3] COLLECTIVE ACTION:
THE "HISTORICAL BLOC IN POWER"

[6.3.1] As Antonio Gramsci, writing from prison, states with the utmost clarity: "If the ruling class has lost consensus, that is, if it no longer 'leads' but only 'rules'—it possesses sheer coercive power [*forza coercitiva*]—this actually means that the great masses have become detached from traditional ideologies, they no longer believe what they previously used to believe."[46]

[6.3.2] The great Italian thinker expresses in these short lines the entirety of the problem I hope to propose. In a given historical moment, there exists a certain social organization of sectors, classes, and groups that, once allied, become a "historic bloc in power." We should think through each component of this phrase.

[6.3.3] First, it is a *bloc*, which indicates an unstable unity that is able to dissolve and recompose itself rapidly.

[6.3.4] Second, it is *historical*, conjunctural, and temporary: it is able to appear today and dissolve tomorrow. The groups that emancipated Latin America from Spain around 1810 were led by white Creoles united strategically and hegemonically with some of the Spanish-born lower classes, with mestizos, with members of indigenous groups, and with slaves and others, all under the banner of the hegemonic project of "liberty." Each, moreover, gave a particular nuance to this value: slaves saw it as liberation from slavery, the indigenous as the recuperation of their land and communal rights, mestizos as full social participation, poor Spanish as a route out of poverty, and Creoles as separation from colonial dependence upon Spain. Once this liberatory moment was complete—approximately during the period from 1820 to 1830—the hegemonic bloc was organized. A new historical bloc was in power, and the Creoles came to occupy the approximate position that the Spanish bureaucracies had previously held in Latin America. Blocs are constructed conjuncturally, and they dissolve in the same way.

[6.3.5] Third, these blocs are *in power*. They are accordingly situated within institutionalized power (*potestas*), and therefore consist of a group of governors or representatives whose political action can be exercised in an *obediential* (*arrow b* in figure 2) or *fetishized* (*arrow d*) manner. According to Gramsci, if the "dominant" or "ruling" class[47] (or the "historical bloc in power") "has lost consensus"—that is, it has lost *hegemony* and thereby consensus because its demands no longer include those of the majority—then it no longer "leads." In other words, it no longer—through the *virtù* demanded by Machiavelli— directs the torrent of *fortuna*, and this is because it has lost the support of power "from below" (*potentia*): institutional power has lost its grounding, and this *potestas* can no longer rely on the capacities of the *people*—their enthusiasm and benevolence. Quite the contrary: upon refusing to participate in the *consensus*, the *people* have shifted toward a position of *dissensus* vis-à-vis the "traditional ideology," an ideology that grounded the obedience of the *people* on the ruling power and that is thereby consensual in the Weberian sense.

[6.3.6] Having lost this consensus, nothing remains for the "historic bloc in power" but political action as "coercive force," and as a result it shifts from being "hegemonic"—having the consent of the *people*—to being "dominant." Domination as political action, which is expressed as a merely monopolistic (military or police), violent, and external force, manifests the crisis of and marks the beginning of the end for the "historical bloc." Anti-popular repression is a sign of having lost power over the institutions of oppression.

7

THE NEED FOR POLITICAL INSTITUTIONS: THE MATERIAL SPHERE (ECOLOGICAL, ECONOMIC, CULTURAL): FRATERNITY

[7.0.1] The institutional *level* (B) contains three *spheres* of institutional organization. The first *sphere* of institutions functionalizes the production and enhancement of the *content* of political institutions and actions [» 7.3, 18] (*M* in figure 3). The second *sphere* is that of the procedural-normative institutions of legitimation [» 8, 1–2, 19] (*L* in figure 3). The third *sphere* is that of the institutions that allow the feasible or concrete empirical instantiation of the other spheres [» 8.3, 20] (*F* in figure 3). Always keep in mind these *three institutional spheres* of *level B* of politics.

[7.1] THE SOCIAL, THE CIVIL, AND THE POLITICAL

[7.1.1] If the private and the public are degrees of *intersubjectivity*, then the social, the civil, and the political are degrees of the *institutionality* of actions or systems within the political field.

[7.1.2] Politics has to do fundamentally with "the social," despite Arendt's erroneous denial of this fact. In the final instance, the objectives of the *content* or the *matter* of politics are the satisfaction of social demands, whether these are in the past and already institutionalized or in the future and still unresolved, thereby giving rise to the need for institutional transformation. The social is the sphere or subfield of the political field that is traversed by the *material* fields (see

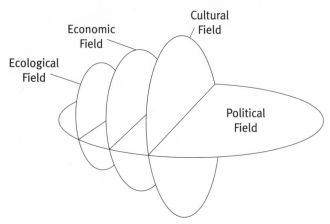

Figure 4. THE MATERIAL FIELDS THAT INTERSECT WITH THE POLITICAL FIELD
*Notes: The political field is traversed by various other fields—in this
case material ones: ecological, economic, and cultural. There are many
other types of fields.*

figure 4)—that is, the ecological, economic, and cultural fields, etc. put into
motion by New Social Movements—in which the realization by actors of
unfulfilled demands produces a crisis (in which the "social problem" appears).
Fundamentally, politics needs to resolve that "social problem."

[7.1.3] "The civil," in turn, has two ambiguous meanings. First, the civil is
the nonpolitical, and in this case the subject is an actor in other practical
fields.[48] In a certain manner, the modern distinction of a "state of nature"
indicates that the political actor existed *before* and *outside* of the political field:
he or she is not merely a citizen. Second, the civil is distinguished from the
political by the latter's high degree of political-institutional systematicity. In
this sense, I will speak of Civil Society (Gramsci's expanded State) and Political Society (the State in the restricted sense). The "civil state" and the "political
state" in modern philosophy up to the eighteenth century—from Hobbes to
Kant—meant essentially the same thing, and both tended to refer to the
sphere of the State (the Leviathan).

[7.1.4] "The political," in relation to the social and the civil, is on the one
hand that same Civil Society, which for Gramsci involved a high degree of

political importance, including culture and institutions among other "civil" classifications, like private universities, communication media, some religious communities, etc. In this sense, every citizen is a political actor. But in the restricted sense, the political can be reserved for the highest institutional level of *potestas*, thanks to whose mediations (Political Society or the State, its government, and its bureaucracies) elected representatives can exercise delegated power.

[7.2] POLITICAL INSTITUTIONS IN GENERAL

[7.2.1] In a certain sense political action [» 6] is a precise, contingent, and perishable moment. Through repetition in time and the systematization of the political field, such actions become *deposited* and *coagulated* in institutions, whose totality we have deemed *potestas*, in distinction from the State [» 8.3, 20]. These institutions both accumulate the achievements of past strategic actions and serve as the condition for future actions. Institutions are conditioned[49] and conditioning[50] conditions, as Marx said of production in the *Grundrisse*.

[7.2.2] For the extreme anarchist, every institution always represents repression, oppression, and injustice. For the conservative, all institutions are everlasting and untouchable. For a critical and realistic politics, institutions are *necessary* despite their imperfection; they are entropic and as such there *always* arises a moment in which they need to be transformed, changed, or destroyed.

[7.2.3] There exists something like a diachrony of institutions, with respect to the degrees of fulfillment of their functions. (a) At birth, institutions respond to neglected demands, and they organize through these demands the enhancement of life and legitimacy. They serve to *discipline* or limit all effective action (like Machiavelli's dikes). (b) In their classical period, that of equilibrium, institutions perform their function adequately, but they also begin to produce an inert weight that tends to perpetuate itself in a nonfunctional way. (c) In the period of institutional crisis, the institution becomes bureaucratic, self-referential, oppressive, and nonfunctional. It becomes necessary to transform or abolish it. Institutional fetishism becomes attached to the institution as if it were an end in itself.

[7.2.4] Freud believed that "culture is the postponement of desire," in the sense that the desire to sleep—for example, of a farm worker—needs to be disciplined, interrupted, and postponed in order for that worker to be able to wake up early to work the field. But the pain of early rising is preferable to the hunger of the hunter-gatherer. The discipline of the farmer entails a certain degree of pain, but the hunger pains of those who are forced to look for food all day without any certainty is even greater. The institution of agriculture postpones the desire to eat all the seeds (leaving some to plant next year's crop), and the same can be said of the desire to sleep longer, the desire to wander the plains as a nomad, etc. But this *discipline*—which Foucault would seem to condemn—is useful for life and necessary for its qualitative improvement. This is moment (a) of the institution. But when the pain produced by that institution reaches such a degree—especially when this pain takes the form of domination or repression, as in the case of the liberal State that forces workers under capitalism to respect a legal system that limits or oppresses them in order to fulfill the pleasure of others[51]—when the suffering it causes is such that the satisfaction it produces is not sufficient to compensate, this means that the moment of transformation has arrived.

[7.2.5] There exist at least three spheres of political institutions. First is the sphere leading to the production, reproduction, and enhancement of the lives of the citizenry. This is the *content* of all political action and therefore I call it *material*.[52] In this case the political field intersects with the ecological, economic, and cultural fields, etc. Second is the sphere of institutions that guarantee the legitimacy of the actions and institutions of the rest of the political system. This is the *formal*, or procedural-normative sphere, and it represents the intersection of the systems of law, the military, the police, the prisons, etc. Third is the sphere of political feasibility, in which institutions allow for the execution of the *content* through reference to the sphere of *legitimacy*. This is, in the final instance, the State administration, but it also includes many other institutions of Civil Society and the social.

[7.3.1] Under liberalism, politics does not look after the economic (it is laissez faire), because this field possesses such a complex logic that it is better for human hands not to interfere with it (the divine "invisible hand" is sufficient to produce the necessary market equilibrium). The minimal State proposed by, for example, Nozick also reduces politics to a minimum, and thereby represents a sort of right-wing anarchism. This is the fulfillment of individual economic freedom, the postulated ideal of Modernity.

[7.3.2] For standard Marxism, in contrast, the economic realm should be completely planned through political organs, thereby achieving a full *rationalization* of the economy in advance without a market (such rationalization represents another postulated ideal of Modernity). The planning State results in the elimination of politics, since the sphere of democratic legitimacy disappears along with the disappearance of the autonomous and free intervention of the citizens, in a reasonable discussion of options to arrive at agreements that subjectively obligate adhesion to a shared consensus. The effort toward total planning reduces politics to *administration* (to instrumental reason), and destroys the *institution* of the market, which, while it never produces equilibrium (and therefore a certain degree of minimal, intelligent, strategic intervention remains necessary in the guise of democratic planning), is necessary nevertheless.

[7.3.3] The political field and its systems always intersect with the *ecological* field and its systems. Until very recently politics had not discovered its ecological responsibilities, but in reality this is its essential function from the very beginning. Politics is an activity that serves the production, reproduction, and enhancement of the life of its citizens, an enhancement that is above all qualitative. Today, it is principally the economic system—on its technological level—that is putting the possibility of mere *bare life* into crisis (to change the meaning of Agamben's phrase *nuda vita*). Assuring the permanence of the life of the population of every nation of humanity on planet Earth is the first and fundamental function of politics, and this criterion of survival must be imposed as the essential criterion of all else. The extinguishing of humanity would obviously annihilate the political field and all of its possible systems. Survival is the *absolute* condition of the rest, and yet there is little normative understanding of the gravity of the situation. We need to create pertinent institutions.

[7.3.4] The political field always intersects with the *economic* field and its systems. This has always been known, since slavery and the use of simple irrigation systems and since the mercantile and agricultural trade of Mesopotamia, the fertile Egyptian Nile, the Indus and Yellow rivers, and the Texcoco and Titicaca lakes. All political systems have been aware of the central importance of the economy. Politics needs to direct the activities of a concrete system in the economic field toward the common good. We need not confuse the economic field with the capitalist economic system, as the latter is merely one possible finite form, and one that will necessarily come to an end and be replaced by forms that operate more efficiently toward the survival of humanity. For the moment, what is necessary is to discover the relations that exist between both fields and their systems. The liberal political system was born as a necessary condition for the capitalist system in England, as we have already indicated. Other systems are possible in both fields, and these become necessary upon discovering the catastrophic and unintentional negative effects of the present economic system. Politics has a certain responsibility.

[7.3.5] The political field inevitably intersects with the *cultural* field (and its systems and subsystems, including religion). This aspect has been very much overlooked by the Left, which has instead given absolute primacy to the economic. In the beginning of 2006 the indigenous president of Bolivia, Evo Morales, defined his political projects as a "Cultural Revolution" (and it certainly has been so). The inclusion of cultural identities—the affirmation of their difference, their diversity—was emphasized by the Sandinista Revolution (thanks to Ernesto Cardenal), by the Zapatista Revolution (through the glorification of Mayan culture), and by the so-called coca farmers of Bolivia. The dimension of narratives and religious rites needs to be included as equally constitutive and central aspects of ancestral cultures (or what Ricoeur calls their "ethico-mythical nucleus"). At the same time, the old critique of ideology has been taken up as a critique of teleology, as suggested by Schmitt but carried out in Latin America principally by Hinkelammert, bearing in mind the political importance of the theology of liberation as a narrative that provides a basis for the praxis of the *people* in Latin America.

[7.3.6] Political institutions need to know how to respond to the claims of these material fields, and they are responsible for providing a certain degree of management and ordering within them. It is not for nothing that all States have secretaries or ministers for the environment, the economy (dealing with currency, tariffs, treasury, central banking, etc.), for education, and occasionally for culture, religious affairs, etc. That is, politics intervenes in all material fields *as* politics and not as an actor capable of developing the specific functions of each material field.

[7.3.7] *Fraternity* is a form of friendship (as Derrida teaches)[53] that unites wills and provides solidity for power. It also stands as an unfulfilled postulate of the bourgeois Revolution of 1789.

INSTITUTIONS IN THE SPHERES OF DEMOCRATIC LEGITIMACY AND FEASIBILITY: EQUALITY AND LIBERTY: GOVERNABILITY

[8.1] THE "FORMAL" SPHERE OF DEMOCRATIC LEGITIMACY

[8.1.1] I refer to as "formal" the sphere that deals with the *form* or *procedure* necessary for an action or institution—and the decisions resulting from either —to be legitimate. That which is considered as *valid* in ethics is subsumed under politics as *legitimate*. For these practical mediations to be legitimate it is necessary, ideally, for all citizens to be able to participate in some symmetrical manner, through reason rather than violence, in the formation of consensus and the agreements that are made. In this sense, the sphere of legitimacy is the proper realm of practical, discursive reason, in a manner similar to that of Apel or Habermas. Legitimacy, then, fortifies the moment of the *unity* of wills through consensus.

[8.1.2] During the last five thousand years—at least since the Phoenician cities in the eastern Mediterranean—political communities have been inventing *institutions* that allowed for the creation of mediations between the political community as a whole and its leaders, who are necessarily much fewer in number. "Institutional systems of legitimation" came about slowly through factors including representation, discussion according to rules (with voting and other instruments) in organs that decide and decree laws, the appearance of codes in which definite behaviors begin to be stipulated as worthy of reward or punishment, the formation of quasi-political bodies to apprehend offenders, the oversight of judges with the authority to pass judgment, and overcoming the barbarous and savage law of "an eye for an eye"—which predated all law and was based on vengeance and "taking justice into one's own hands."

[8.1.3] From among the diverse systems of government (monarchies and republics), *democracy* came to emerge as the only feasible form for the achievement of legitimacy. Today, the task is to assess and improve upon the various types of democracy: republican, liberal, social democratic, welfare State, postcolonial populist, etc. Existing *empirical* democratic systems are always concrete, inimitable in their entirety by other States, and always open for improvement. Democracy is a perpetually unfinished system.

[8.1.4] Democracy is not merely a *procedural* system—a simple form for arriving at consensus—but instead also is *normative*. The fact of always seeking an increased symmetry and participation among citizens—never perfect, always perfectible—is not merely an *external* or *legal* conduct, as might derive from some of Kant's texts or those of Bobbio. It is, to the contrary, a subjective obligation on the part of the citizen who has promulgated certain laws in a community to determine behavior, laws that then require obedience given the citizen's participation in their promulgation: *Pacta servanda sunt* ("pacts should be fulfilled"). Those having made a pact are, by definition, those who must fulfill it, and it would be a performative contradiction to provide laws for others that do not apply to those who create them. Obedience to the law is not *external*—purely legal or procedural—but rather is subjective and normative, because the political actor who is sovereign to decree the law must also be obedient in its fulfillment. The delegated exercise of *obediential* power, in turn, also fulfills the law, but with an even firmer obligation to *obey the community* as its representative [» 4.2].

[8.2] THE LEGAL SYSTEM AND "GOVERNMENT BY LAW": EQUALITY

[8.2.1] The system of political legitimacy has as its central reference point the "legal system" in the broadest sense. See the position of this *system* in figure 5.

[8.2.2] When undifferentiated power (*potentia*) decides to organize itself institutionally, the delegated exercise of power is determined (*arrow a* in figure 5) first as instituted power (*potestas*), which then, with respect to a possible Constitution, becomes a constituent power (which is concretized as a Constit-

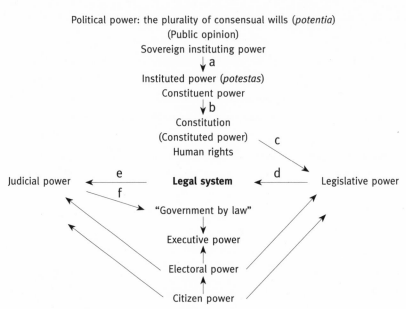

Figure 5. SOME ASPECTS OF THE INSTITUTIONALITY OF THE STATE
WITH RESPECT TO THE FORMAL SPHERE

uent Assembly, *arrow b*). This *Constitution*, which should promulgate *Human Rights*, in turn and necessarily establishes (*arrow c*) an organ to create laws. It is in this way that *Legislative Power* is born, which permanently promulgates and actualizes (*arrow d*) the *legal system* in a constitutional manner. *Judicial Power,*[54] in turn, interprets the legal system and *applies* it in concrete cases, resolving conflicts that had appeared in the political community (*arrow f*). All of these levels—which become a stable, consensual, and ultimately normative habitual practice within the political community—create a "government by law." That same *Executive Power* (which will enter into the sphere of feasibility [» 8.3]) acts legitimately and administratively within the legal frame. *Electoral Power,*[55] in turn, prepares the registers and lists of candidates, and judges the legitimacy of the electoral processes of all the other Powers and institutions (political and civil, if the latter are required). *Citizen Power* is the last instance of control over all other Powers and institutions, and it should be the culmination of an entire permanent process of participation by the members of the community from their base. These complex relationships require a more detailed discussion that I will complete in due course.[56]

[8.2.3] For its part, the bourgeois Revolution of 1789 proposed a procedural-normative postulate: *Equality*. However, this postulate would prove empirically impossible to implement. This was not only due to the intrinsic impossibility of all postulates, but moreover, because the Revolution rested on a capitalist system in the economic field. Instead of situating the citizenry according to an increasing degree of symmetry, throughout the two centuries since its formulation these social asymmetries have grown immensely. Since this *Equality* was not achieved, this failure calls into question the very legitimacy of modern, liberal, bourgeois democracy.

[8.3] THE INSTITUTIONS OF POLITICAL "FEASIBILITY": CIVIL AND POLITICAL SOCIETY: FREEDOM AND GOVERNABILITY

[8.3.1] Institutions as such are mediations of feasibility. They "make possible" (*feasible*) the use of appropriate means to accomplish assigned ends, and as such they could be considered an exercise of instrumental or strategic power as formulated by Weber or Horkheimer. But in a stricter sense in the political field and in all political systems, it is necessary to have more than material institutions (to reproduce and enhance the life of the citizen) and institutions of legitimacy (to operate within a mutually accepted consensus). Also necessary are administrative instruments that allow the fulfillment of the specified goals of the other two spheres (the material and formal spheres mentioned above). This is the sphere of political feasibility.

[8.3.2] For example, without a system for collecting resources (taxes) it would not be possible to finance all of the necessary political institutions. A country that is immensely rich in a technical and economic sense will have more resources than a poor one, and as such politics will have more potential (feasibility) from the outset to accomplish its goals. We have seen that *feasibility* is one of the determinations of power as such [» 2.3], and thus if there is no instrumental or administrative feasibility—which includes, for example, a defensive and popular military force—then the community in question will lack sufficient power to be governable.

[8.3.3] The micro-institutions of political feasibility—whose public ends are particular—include both institutions within *Civil Society* (including private schools, religious communities, communication media, etc.) and also those that cross the threshold of the merely social and penetrate into the properly political sphere of the State (but here in the broad sense, following Gramsci).

[8.3.4] The macro-institution of feasibility is *Political Society* or the State (in the restricted sense), whose universal ends comprise the entire political community, and which has seen a long process of institutionalization during the past five millennia.[57] The five Powers already alluded to form part of the State, as do the police, the army, institutions of public education, certain State-owned enterprises, etc.

[8.3.5] This entire structure of the political system functions to make political life within the political field *governable*. *Governability* is a virtue of a system and is fundamentally ambiguous. Without governability there can be no political life, but in the presence of a fetishized governability [» 5] stable political life is also impossible in the long term. The expression "the governability of democracy" can be understood as a cynical one[58] in the sense that democratic legitimacy is not the final instance of judgment but rather there exists a *higher* evaluative moment: one that is no longer that of the political community itself but instead that of a foreign, metropolitan, imperial, military power.

[8.3.6] It is within this sphere of feasibility that the bourgeois postulate of *liberty* can be located (the "first principle" of Rawls). This faculty (and right) allows the citizen to work autonomously and without impediment, choosing what is best. However, poverty, for example, impedes the needier citizens ("the social problem") from operating freely, because they lack the objective possibility to intervene in public life, pursued as they are by everyday vulnerability.

[8.3.7] In the spheres of democratic legitimacy and feasibility, "public opinion" plays an irreplaceable function. "Public opinion" penetrates the totality of the political body, as the "hermeneutic" (interpretive) moment of all aspects of life in the political field, and this gives it its ontological centrality: public opinion is like the prediscursive precomprehension of the political[59] (which cannot be left without juridical regulation in the hands of private trans-nationals, whose alleged "business" is news and "entertainment"). Politics as "spectacle"—rather than as "participation" and as a "culture" that entails the education of the *people*—is the *corruption* of politics through information, which leads us toward mediaocracy. Political power, fetishized by money, penetrates all of the interstices of the political systems, inverting them and placing them in the service of power *as domination* [» 5]. It is in this way that the political community can become alienated.

ETHICS AND THE IMPLICIT NORMATIVE PRINCIPLES OF POLITICS: THE MATERIAL PRINCIPLE

[9.1] ETHICS AND POLITICAL NORMATIVITY

[9.1.1] The relationship between ethics and politics has, in various ways, been posed inadequately. The first way is as a nonrelation between ethics (as the subjective obligation of the individual) and politics (which remains determined externally, legally, or coercively). This is more or less Kant's position. In a certain sense politics understood in this manner loses all normativity and its rules become purely procedural or "Machiavellian."

[9.1.2] Others argue that there exists a "political ethic," but in a way this solution is as ambiguous as the first. The principles of this political ethic are ethical, and politics as such can be exercised without such extrinsic principles.

[9.1.3] The position of Apel and Habermas, on the other hand, attempts to show how abstract moral-discursive principles can be applied to the democratic principle or to law. In this case, at least normativity is salvaged, but they fall into a formalism (there are only formal political principles: democracy and law).

[9.1.4] Solutions to the difficulties inherent in political ethics, then, vary. It is necessary to accept that ethics has universal normative principles,[60] but also that it lacks its own practical field, since no act can be *purely* ethical. An individual always operates within a concrete practical field, whether it be economic, political, pedagogical, sporting, familial, cultural, etc. On the other hand, ethical *obligation* is exercised *distinctly* in each practical field. The obligation of "Thou shalt not kill" (ethical *similarity*) is exercised in the political field as "Thou shalt not kill your political antagonist." This is the *normativity* (duty, requirement, obligation) of the political field, and it is analogous to ethical normativity, which represents the primary abstract analogate. Political principles *subsume* ethical principles, *incorporate* them, and then *transform* them to political normativity (see figure 6).

[9.1.5] Political principles are, on the other hand, *intrinsic to* and *constitutive of potentia* [» 2] (the power of the community) as well as of *potestas* [» 3] (the delegated exercise of power), since each determination of power is the result of a political *obligation* that functions as a duty constraining the actions of actors and their fulfillment of the function of institutions. Political principles constitute, fortify, and regenerate the system *from within*, forcing the agents to affirm the Will-to-Live in the feasible consensus of the entire community, and to act with an eye to hegemony (as obediential power) and encouraging the fulfillment of the tasks of each institutional sphere [» 7–8, 17–20] (material, formal legitimacy, and efficient feasibility).

[9.1.6] A political actor who fails to fulfill the normative principles of politics is not only (subjectively) unjust, *but also contributes to the weakening and rotting of power* and of the actions and institutions through which he or she seeks to govern. The fetishism of power [» 5.1]—which is the nonfulfillment of political normativity—is self-destructive and isolates delegated power (*potestas*) from its source (*potentia*).

[9.2] THE THREE "IMPLICIT" PRINCIPLES

[9.2.1] Political principles operate *implicitly*, like the grammatical rules that a mother teaches her child despite knowing little about grammar—for example, by correcting the child with regard to the rules of concordance between the genders of nouns and adjectives.[61] In the same way, all political actors in the realm of politics are *implicitly* aware of its principles. However, it is a good idea to *specify* these in order to improve normative consciousness, to be able to teach them more clearly, and to be able to provide them with a foundation.

[9.2.2] There are at least three essential normative principles of politics. The *material* principle (M) (in figure 7) operates with regard to the lives of the citizenry, the *formal* democratic principle (L) determines the duty to always act

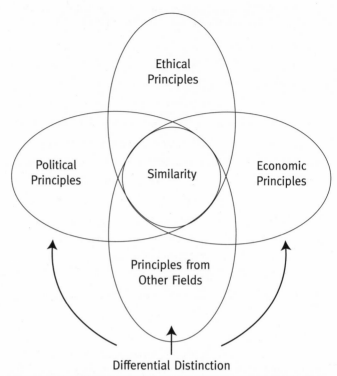

Differential Distinction

Figure 6. THE ANALOGICAL SUBSUMPTION OF ETHICAL PRINCIPLES IN THE POLITICAL FIELD

Notes: In the sphere of Similarity, *the obligatory nature of ethical principles coincides with others (Similarity = Political principles ∩ Economic principles ∩ Other principles). This is done through* similarity, *not* identity *(for example, the ethical expression "Thou shalt not kill" is not the same in every field, but only similar). The level of* Analogical distinction *is where each principle* does not *coincide with others (but in which the differences are not* specific, *but rather* analogated*). Thus in the economic field the analogates say, "Thou shalt not kill [*Similarity*] your competitor in the market [proper to the Economic Principle]." In the political field they say, "Thou shalt not kill [*Similarity*] your antagonist in a struggle for hegemony [in politics]." In other fields they say, for example, "Thou shalt not kill [*Similarity*] your child!" in the field of pedagogy (after all, Abraham did not kill Isaac, whereas the same could not be said in the story of Oedipus); or in the field of gender relations, "Thou shalt not kill [*Similarity*] your wife," and so forth.*

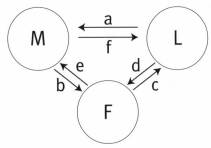

Figure 7. THE MUTUAL CODETERMINATION OF POLITICAL PRINCIPLES
Notes: M is the material sphere; L is the formal, procedural-normative sphere of the system of democratic legitimacy; and F is the sphere of strategic feasibility. Arrows a, b, c, d, e, f indicate the direction of mutual determination without a final instance.

in accordance with the principles proper to democratic legitimacy, and the principle of *feasibility* (F) similarly implies that the actor only work toward the possible (beyond conservative possibility but not quite so far as anarchist possibility).

[9.2.3] These principles, lacking a final instance, are mutually determined, with each serving as the conditioning conditioned condition of the others.

[9.2.4] In the standard Marxist tradition, the material (economic) principle is the last instance. In the liberal tradition, the formal-democratic principle is the last instance. In the cynicism of a politics without principles, feasibility operates without any restriction. Here, I hope to overcome these reductive positions. *Arrow a* (figure 7) indicates the *formal* determination of the democratic legitimacy of all economic, ecological, and cultural actions and institutions. *Arrow f*, on the other hand, indicates the *material* determination of democratic actions and institutions, and so on.[62] We are dealing, then, with complex, mutual codetermination, which lacks a final instance.

[9.3] THE POLITICO-MATERIAL PRINCIPLE

[9.3.1] All modern European political philosophy has always presupposed the *material* principle that I hope to point out here. Hobbes explains in the *Leviathan* (1642) that in the "state of nature" individuals establish a continuous state of war, and some kill others. For *life to be possible*, then, it is necessary to establish a pact, and with it the "civil state," to ensure survival. This reasoning lies equally behind the arguments of Spinoza, Locke, and Rousseau, and it presupposes that political institutions are premised on the possibility of the stable production, reproduction, and enhancement of the lives of the citizens of a political community (*potestas* [» 3]).

[9.3.2] Here, *material* does not mean something physical but refers instead to *content*, as when one says "The content or material that I explain in this book is politics." In this sense, the *content* (or the *material*) of all politics (of its actions, institutions, etc.) is in the last instance human life, the concrete lives of each person, or a sort of "bare life" that is more concrete than Agamben's *nuda vita*. All political actions or institutions have as their content some reference to life. Agriculture produces nourishment for life. Roads shorten the distance we must cross to fulfill functions that always refer in the end to some dimension of human life. Politics deals with creating the conditions of possibility for and advancement of the life of the community and each of its members: a possible life, a qualitatively better life. As Johann Fichte writes: "The objective of all human [political] activity is *to be able to live*, and all those who nature has brought *to life* have the same right to this *possibility of living*. For this reason, it is necessary to make the division above all so that all have access to the means sufficient to their survival. *Live and let live!*"[63]

[9.3.3] So, a minimal description of this material principle could be enunciated as follows: We should always operate so that the norms or maxims guiding all our actions, all organizations or institutions (micro or macro), all delegated exercise of obediential power, have as their purpose the *production, maintenance, and enhancement of the immediate lives* of the citizens of the political community, in the last instance all of humanity, being also responsible for these objectives in the medium and long term (the next few millennia).[64] As such, political action and institutions can have a *political claim toward practical truth*, which would take the form in the ecological subsphere of the maintenance and augmentation of the general life of the planet, in the economic subsphere of the permanence and development of production, distribution, and exchange of material goods, and in the cultural subsphere of the conservation of identity and growth of the linguistic, aesthetic, religious, theoretical, and practical content of the corresponding cultural traditions. The *satisfaction* of the needs of the living corporeality of the citizenry—in ecological, economic, and cultural terms—will prove *as an empirical fact* the achievements of the governor's political justice claim. This is a principle with a universal claim, whose only limits are the planet Earth and humanity as a whole, at present and even into the distant future.

[9.3.4] Politics is above all that action that aspires toward the advancement of the life of the community, of the *people*, of humanity!

THE FORMAL-DEMOCRATIC AND FEASIBILITY
PRINCIPLES OF POLITICS

[10.0.1] Table 2 depicts the complexity of the structural order of the three architectonic *levels* suggested above [» 6.01], from the point of view of normative principles, of political postulates [» 17.3], of political utopias, of concrete political systems, of political projects as the ends of action, and so on.

[10.0.2] All thirteen of these distinctions will need to be described, not only in this volume but also in my works forthcoming.[65] For now, however, they are useful as a point of reference for the text that follows.

[10.1] THE DEMOCRATIC PRINCIPLE

[10.1.1] *Democracy*, essentially, is an institutionalization of those mediations that allow *legitimate* decisions, actions, institutions, and delegated exercise of power. These are implemented through systems of empirical institutions that are invented, tested, and corrected by humanity throughout the millennia in order to achieve a strong measure of approval by the citizenry. The purpose of this is the forging of a legitimate consensus [» 8.1]. This entire institutional system is constituted and encouraged *from within* by a normative principle, which subsumes the universal *validity principle* of ethics in the political field. *Validity* in ethics is analogous to *legitimacy* in politics, and the latter adds to mere ethical validity the existence of coercive institutions over which *potestas*

Table 2. VARIOUS LOGICAL DEGREES OF ABSTRACTION AND THE APPLICATIONS OF PRINCIPLES,
TELEOLOGICAL MOMENTS, AND ACTIONS, AND THEIR EFFECTS ON A GIVEN POLITICAL ORDER.

Level C: Political Principles

1. Ontological order or *omnitudo realitatis*	- Ontological foundation or real constitution of the living human
2. *Implicit* ethical principles	- First degree of abstraction
3. *Implicit* political principles	- Subsumes the previous level
4. Political postulates	- Statements of perfection
5. Political utopias and paradigms	- Imagined with historical content

Level B: Political Institutions

6. Concrete, historical political system	- Institutions are shaped according to principles, postulates, projects, etc.

Level A: Political Action

7. Political projects and the goals of actions	- Goals of concrete action are organized
8. Strategic rules of action	- Determined based on decided goals
9. Tactical rules of action	- Determined conjuncturally by strategy
10. Political means to be employed	- Selected from among tactics
11. Concrete political action (*praxis*)	- Decided as a result and enacted contingently

Positive or negative political effects

12. Short-term, unintentional	- Follow actions immediately
13. Long-term, unintentional	- Difficult to foresee

Notes: Political utopias are not normative political "principles," but rather regulative ideas that orient the level of political action (A. and the correction of its negative effects, levels 12–13). I would like to distinguish between utopias (which are narratives like that of Thomas More) and models or paradigms of political systems like the liberal system, the welfare state, neoliberal or socialist systems, etc. Statements of perfection are similar to Kant's historical or political postulates, regulative ideals, or criteria of orientation. These are Hinkelammert's "transcendental concepts" [»17.3]. The entire critical discourse of political philosophy develops out of these negative political effects, which is the subject of part 2 [»13.1].

holds a monopoly, in the absence of which every individual might attempt to resolve the injustices they suffer through vengeance: we would find ourselves in a state of barbarity on the order of that which predated all government by law.

[10.1.2] The *democratic principle* is frequently present in the work of the modern philosophers, but this alone does not prevent them from falling into certain ambiguities. For example, Rousseau writes, in the *Social Contract*, that it is necessary "to find a *form of association* which may defend and protect with the whole force of the community the person and property of every associate, and by means of which each, coalescing with all, may nevertheless obey only himself, and remain as free as before."[66]

[10.1.3] This formulation contains many ambiguities. First, this *form of association*—the procedural *form*—needs not only to defend every person but must also primarily defend the entire community, because the point of departure is not isolated individuals but rather *always already* presupposed historical communities. A Robinson Crusoe who does not *become* lost but is instead always already isolated could not even be born! This is a contradiction. One could not even develop into a human in solitude: how, for example, would one learn how to speak? The community always exists as a point of departure. Second, and as a result, when the citizen participates symmetrically—reaching consensus through giving reasons—he or she does indeed "coalesce with all" while "nevertheless obey[ing] only himself," since laws are freely decided upon and therefore entail an *obligation* as a result of self-legislation. But in this case citizens do not remain "as free *as before*," because now they are bound by an obligation of citizenship that constitutes them as free but does so within a juridical order of *fraternity* that prevents unrestrained spontaneity. Freedom is now communicative, and it can be exercised *legitimately* if it obeys self-dictated law, provided symmetrical participation in the institutionalization of that law.

[10.1.4] Democracy is fundamentally a normative principle (item 3 in table 2), a sort of obligation that applies *within* the space of the (always intersubjective) subjectivity of every citizen and that stimulates from within all architectonic moments of politics. A minimal description of this is presented below.

[10.1.5] We should always operate politically in such a way that all decisions regarding all action, all organization, or all structures of a (micro or macro) institution—on the material level, in the formal legal system (like the passing of a law), or in the realm of juridical application, that is, in the delegated exercise of obediential power—be the result of a process of agreement by consensus in which *the affected can participate* in the fullest way possible (insofar as we are aware). Moreover, this agreement must be decided *through reasonable discussion* (without violence) with the *highest possible degree of symmetry* among participants, taking place publicly and according to the (democratic) institutional structure agreed upon beforehand. A decision thus taken is imposed upon the community and upon each member as a *political duty*, which *legitimately obligates* the citizen in a normative and practical way (thereby subsuming formal, moral principles as political).[67]

[10.1.6] This principle is operative from the very first moment in which the community decides to institutionalize itself (even prior to there being a constitution), and it should be fulfilled without exception in *every moment* of the unfolding and development of *all political processes*. Democratic centralism (a contradictory squared circle), the governability of Imperial democracy, or governing as a minority (through tricking the majority with apparent legitimacy, be it Weberian or liberal)—these notions must all be rejected and overcome through continuous attention to the realization of this normative principle. From *behind the closed doors* (that is, in the nonpublic realm) of the elite practice of bourgeois power, in the State Department or the Central Committee, legitimate and democratic agreements can never be reached. This is the greatest lesson of the misfortunes of real existing socialism.

[10.2] IMPLEMENTATION OF THE DEMOCRATIC PRINCIPLE

[10.2.1] All principles must be applied empirically. The ancients referred to "practical wisdom" as *prudence* (*phronesis* in Greek), which inclined the citizen to *know how to apply* universal principles correctly to concrete cases. The universality of a principle does not eliminate, but rather only clarifies, the inevitable uncertainty of all political decisions, and as a result it is always fallible. At present, without rejecting that position we must integrate it intersubjectively, by which I mean that *application* to the concrete case be collective according to the democratic principle (through symmetrical participation by the affected, who give reasons in order to arrive at agreements). But communities can never, or only in exceptional cases, arrive at unanimity, and as a result there will always be *minorities* in disagreement and in dissensus. Here we need to be conscious of the various instruments used to apply the principle, none of which is democratic in itself *if not internally animated by the normative principle qua normative* (*that is, as a subjective obligation for the citizens*).

[10.2.2] No decision is *perfect*, as this would require infinite intelligence, pure fraternity, and unlimited time—all things that are impossible in light of human finitude. All decisions—which constrain actions and found institutions—are accordingly *not perfect*, that is, they are imperfect and as such will *always* result in some unintentional negative effects (items 12 and 13 in table 2). For the most part, it is the *minorities* or the opposition who grasp these negative effects since they are the ones who suffer from them, and it is in the resolution of these negative effects that we find the future, the transformation, and the *qualitative* progress of life. To respect the minority is to respect the future; it is to accept the possibility of inevitable mistakes and then be able to correct such mistakes through the same normative principles discussed above.

[10.2.3] All votes to close a discussion are by definition an interruption of an unfinished process. As a result, any decision adopted by voting *does not represent the practical truth* but rather only an agreement reached up to a certain moment, and such decisions are thereby imperfect and contain inevitable negative effects. Voting is simply an instrument of human finitude in light of progress toward a future of better decisions.

[10.2.4] Therefore, against Habermas, the monological *prudence* of the singular always has importance because in the end agreement is the organic sum of monological decisions decided by *individual prudence*. Moreover, the dissident—who could be correct, and a source of future progress—believes in her or his proposal *not due to agreement* (because the position is one of a dissident) but rather through her or his singular evaluation of the case in question (in which judgment is therefore prudential). In sum, the communal, discursive, democratic principle does not result in an avoidance of the singular responsibility of all citizens, who should have the courage to express their dissidence when they believe it to be well founded (as a result of each individual's singular political conscience).

[10.2.5] The same can be said of *representation*. Given the impossibility of direct democracy, it is necessary to elect representatives. The free and secret election of representatives is an institution that was invented long ago. It is not identical to a *perfect* election, neither is it intrinsically *democratic*. Rather, it is an institutional moment that, encouraged by the democratic principle, functions alongside other mediating institutions that are *not exempt from the possibility of corruption*.

[10.2.6] The totality of the liberal democratic system, for example, is equally a concrete system (item 6 in table 2): in no way should it be considered a normative principle or even an example to imitate. It is the result of a historical process carried out successfully by *every colonialist metropolitan community* (England, France, the United States, etc.). Peripheral and postcolonial democratic systems need to study concrete institutions that are democratic from the outset in order to create new, feasible, and appropriate concrete systems.[68]

[10.3] THE POLITICAL PRINCIPLE OF STRATEGIC FEASIBILITY

[10.3.1] We now reach a central theme of politics, to which Machiavelli granted considerable importance in *Il Principe*. Politics has been defined by some as "the art of the possible," which refers to an empirical *possibility*—but one of a very specific type. Its limit is the *impossible*. Hegel tells us of *impossible* political projects when he points out that "these abstractions . . . afforded the tremendous spectacle . . . of the overthrow of all existing and given conditions within an actual major state . . . to give it what was *supposed* to be a purely *rational* basis."[69] Marx, on the other hand, shows the *impossibility* of politics (and of capitalism itself) when left in the hands of mercantile relations, which sacrifice human life exclusively to the progress of capital. This position is formulated by Hinkelammert as follows: "Capitalist society is *impossible* because it is self-destructive, and as a result the progress unleashed within bourgeois society can only be oriented toward *human life*."[70]

[10.3.2] This "management" of an action or an institution (capital, after all, is also an institution) indicates the normative moment of the principle of feasibility, now operating in the political field, which is nothing more than the process of containing systemic, efficient action within the parameters of the other two normative political principles already enunciated.

[10.3.3] The normative principle of political feasibility could be described approximately as follows: We should operate strategically, bearing in mind that political actions and institutions must always be considered as *feasible possibilities*, which are *beyond* mere conservative possibility (item 1 in table 3) but *fall short* of the impossible-possibility of the extreme anarchist (item 3 in table 3), whether from the Right in the case of Nozick or from the Left in the case of

Bakunin. In other words, the successful means and ends of actions and institutions should be achieved within the "strict framework" suggested by Luxemburg, where *content* is delimited and motivated from within by the material political principle (the *immediate life* of the community), and where *legitimacy* has come to be determined by the democratic principle. The same works for the means, tactics, and strategies used to fulfill those ends within the concrete political project being attempted (items 7–11 in table 2).[71] The "political feasibility claim" of strategic action, then, should fulfill the material and formal normative conditions in each of its steps (which I established in the text above). But moreover, through its own demands of political *efficacy* in the management of scarcity and governability, it allows the normative feasibility of power to give rise to a political order that in the long run achieves permanence and stability. This results not only from directing its actions toward *positive* effects (worthy of merit and honor) but especially from taking responsibility for *negative* effects (worthy of critique or punishment). By always attempting to correct these negative effects, while indirect or unintentional,[72] the hope is that they will not produce definitively irreversible facts. Toward this end, strategic feasibility must consider the notion of efficiency with regard to the use of scarce resources (which are quantitatively finite in contrast to a community with growing needs), as well as the notion of governability (through the complexity of institutions), which always sets out from the contingent uncertainty of the undecidable element of actions and institutions.

Table 3. THREE TYPES OF POLITICAL "POSSIBILITY"

1.	2.	3.
Conservative *possibility* (surpassed by the critic)	Critical *possibility* (*impossible* for the conservative; surpassed by the anarchist)	Anarchist *possibility* (*Impossible* for the critic and the conservative)

PART 2

THE CRITICAL TRANSFORMATION OF THE POLITICAL: TOWARD THE NEW POLITICAL ORDER

Not even the best possible empirical political order is perfect. I have already shown how, given the *finite human condition*, such a degree of resolution is *impossible*. This allows us to deduce that, since political orders are imperfect, negative effects are inevitable, and all the more so when we keep in mind the uncertainty of all human action. Those suffering these negative effects are the *victims*—and they are political victims. Because victims cannot live at a level relative to the historical development of humanity, they in some way find themselves participating only asymmetrically in the system, or even are fully excluded from it. In sum, because the political order is unable to distribute the benefits of the current order to everyone, it manifests its ineffectiveness in its victims by the simple fact of their existence as victims.

When suffering becomes unacceptable and intolerable from the perspective of the victims, oppositional social movements emerge within the empirical political field—alongside which critical theories emerge that are organically linked with them. The political philosophy I discuss in part 2 arrives at a point of critique of the prevailing system, thereby beginning a deconstruction of the philosophy laid out in part 1. The central theme of this deconstructive task will be the political victims, who are oppressed, repressed, and excluded, if not also tortured and murdered by all of the "dirty wars" of recent history.

11

THE *PEOPLE*: THE POPULAR SECTOR AND "POPULISM"

[11.1] SOCIAL MOVEMENTS AND HEGEMONIC DEMANDS

[11.1.1] The intersubjective referent of the prevailing political order described in part 1 is what I have deemed the "political community." The notion of *community*, in going beyond the metaphysical individualism of liberalism but falling short of the substantive collectivism of real existing socialism, indicates the originary intersubjective insertion of the singular subjectivity of every citizen. We are born within a political community, which is always already presupposed phylogenetically (as a human species) and ontogenetically (as a singularity). From a political point of view, however, this is still an abstraction lacking the contradictions and conflicts that *always* traverse that community. We ascend, then, from the simple to the complex, from the abstract to the concrete. We now move from the "political community" to the *people.*

[11.1.2] If all sectors of the political community were able to have their demands fulfilled, there would be no social protest or formation of popular movements struggling for the fulfillment of their unsatisfied demands. It is by starting from the *negativity* of needs—for some dimension of life, or for democratic participation—that the *struggle for recognition* is frequently transformed into demand-based mobilizations, which do not await justice as a gift of the powerful but rather seek it as an autonomous achievement of the movements. In this sense, there could exist as many movements as there are differential claims.

[11.1.3] The problem of politics appears when we realize that there exist as many demands as there are needs around which movements are born—such as, for example, feminist movements, anti-racist movements, movements organized by the elderly, by indigenous peoples, by the marginal and unemployed, by the industrial working class, by poor or "landless" farmers, and movements of a geopolitical nature against the colonialist metropole, against Eurocentrism, against militarism, and those for pacifism and for the environment, etc. Each of these movements is based on *differential claims*,[73] which oppose one another in principle. How can these pass from being *a* particular claim to being a *hegemonic* claim able to unify all social movements in a country at a given moment? This is a question of moving from differential particularities to *a universal* one that encompasses them.

[11.1.4] The solution of the passage from each singular claim to *a universal, hegemonic claim* can be found in the proposal offered by Laclau. This process of "passage" is complex, and here I will merely note that it takes the form of univocal equivalence.[74]

[11.1.5] Boaventura de Sousa Santos,[75] on the other hand, believes that each demand must enter into a process of dialogue and *translation*, with the goal of achieving an understanding between movements that nonetheless never represents an encompassing universal. Critical postmodernism gives rise to an open dialogical hermeneutic.

[11.1.6] It would still be possible to think that the demands of movements (1, 2, 3, N in figure 8) progressively incorporate those of other movements into their own. Feminism discovers that women *of color* are treated worst, that female workers receive lower salaries, that female citizens do not occupy positions of representation, that women in peripheral countries suffer even more discrimination, etc. Similarly, the indigenous person discovers the exploitation of the community under capitalism, within the dominant Western culture, in subtle but nevertheless prevalent racism, etc. That is, through mutual information, dialogue, translation of proposals, and shared militant praxis, these movements slowly and progressively constitute an *analogical hegemon*, which to some degree includes all demands but might, according to Laclau, prioritize some. In the process of emancipation from Spain in 1810, "Liberty!" was given an indisputable primacy as a demand that unified all

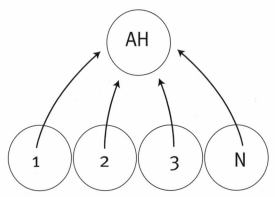

Figure 8. THE PROCESS OF CONSTITUTING AN ANALOGICAL *HEGEMON*
FROM DISTINCTIVE DEMANDS
*Notes: Circles 1, 2, 3, N represent differential identities and
social movements (per Boaventura de Sousa) that constitute a
complex hegemonic demand (AH), with analogical distinctions
according to what is proper to each movement.*

groups into the patriotic bloc of Latin America. The arrows in figure 8 show
out this process of analogical incorporation, which maintains the distinctive-
ness of each movement.

[11.1.7] These movements alongside the critical sectors of the political community—which can include the petty bourgeoisie suffering an unemployment
crisis and the national bourgeoisie destroyed by transnational competition—
construct a "bloc" that comes "from below" with an increasingly developed
national and popular consciousness of the unfulfilled needs and claims that are
assumed with a clear understanding of the demands they entail.

[11.2] THE PEOPLE: THE "PLEBS" AND THE "POPULUS"

[11.2.1] In the process of creating a hegemonic bloc, the need arises for a
category that can encompass the unity of all the movements, classes, sectors,
etc., in political struggle. And so the *people* is that strictly political category[76]
(since it is not properly sociological or economic) that appears as absolutely
essential, despite its ambiguity (and indeed this ambiguity does not result
from misunderstanding but rather from inevitable complexity). In a famous

speech, Fidel Castro addresses the question of the *people* "when we speak of struggle"—that is, when we use the concept of the *people* within the horizon of politics, strategy, and tactics:

> When we speak of struggle and we mention the *people* we mean the vast unredeemed masses . . . those who long for great and wise *changes* in all aspects of their life; the *people* who, to attain those changes, are ready to give even the very last breath they have when they believe in something or in someone,[77] especially *when they believe in themselves.* . . . In terms of struggle, when we talk about the *people* we're talking about the six hundred thousand Cubans *without work*[78] . . . the five hundred thousand *farm laborers* who live in miserable shacks . . . the four hundred thousand *industrial workers and laborers* . . . whose salaries pass from the hands of the boss to those of the moneylender . . . the one hundred thousand small farmers who live and die working land that is not theirs, looking at it with the sadness *of Moses gazing at the promised land*[79] . . . the thirty thousand teachers and professors . . . the twenty thousand small business men weighed down by debts . . . the ten thousand young professional *people* . . . anxious to work and full of hope . . . These are the *people*, the ones who know misfortune and, therefore, are capable of fighting with limitless courage![80]

[11.2.2] In later texts, Castro includes abandoned children, women in patriarchal society, the elderly, etc. In countries like Bolivia, Peru (the home of Mariátegui, who was accused by dogmatic Marxists of being a "populist"), Guatemala, and Mexico, we need to add indigenous ethnic groups. Moreover, as a result of urbanization processes, we should not forget the marginalized masses, the poor and recently arrived immigrants, those who have been expelled politically to the exteriority of the State, etc.

[11.2.3] The Aztec term *altepetl* and the Mayan term *Amaq'* refer to the "community" or the *pueblo*, and even vividly to the "we" that has been forgotten by modern, Western experience.[81] As a result, in Latin America—through the indigenous influence that permeates the continent—the word *pueblo* means something more profound than merely "the *people*" in romance languages.

[11.2.4] The *pueblo* establishes an internal frontier or a fracture within the political community. There can be citizens and members of a State who are nevertheless, according to their relation to the bloc in power, distinguished from the *pueblo*, as is the case with those whose needs remain unsatisfied by oppression or exclusion. We will use the term *plebs* (in Latin) to refer to the *people* when considered in opposition to the elites, to the oligarchs, to the ruling classes of a political order. This term *plebs*, meaning a part of the community, nevertheless tends to encompass all of the citizens (*populus*) in a *new* future order in which their present claims will be satisfied and equality will be achieved thanks to a common struggle by the excluded.

[11.2.5] It is not surprising that Negri opposes the concept of the *multitude* (as he defines it) to that of the *people*, which he views as an inadequate and substantialist concept: "Is it possible today to imagine a new process of legitimation that does not rely on the sovereignty of the *people* but is based instead in the biopolitical productivity of the multitude?"[82] In my opinion the answer is no, but regardless I agree that it is necessary to understand the *people* in an entirely new way.

[11.3] THE "SOCIAL BLOC OF THE OPPRESSED,"
THE POPULAR SECTOR, AND POPULISM

[11.3.1] In this reformulation, the *people* is transformed into a *collective political actor* rather than being merely a substantial and fetishized "historical subject." The *people* appears in critical political conjunctures when it achieves explicit consciousness as the *analogical hegemon* of all demands, from which it defines strategy and tactics, thereby becoming an *actor* and constructing history on the basis of a new foundation. As many social movements note: "Power is constructed from below!"

[11.3.2] Gramsci, in order to avoid this substantialization (of the working class as a "historical subject" in standard Marxism), employs the concept of "bloc." A "bloc" is not hard like a stone but instead represents a whole that can be both integrated and disintegrated. It can have "contradictions" at its very heart (as Mao suggested), and it appears forcefully in a moment and disappears when it has completed its task (that is, if this task is accomplished, since the *people* often fail). It is a "*social* bloc" because it originates from conflicts in the material fields (ecological extinction, economic poverty, the destruction of cultural identity) and then slowly crosses the first threshold of Civil Society; from there it moves to the second threshold of Political Society. These steps were taken by Evo Morales in his progression from leader of the coca farmers' movement to participant in mobilizations of Civil Society to founder of a political party (within Political Society) and then on to his election as president of the Republic of Bolivia. The *people* is a social bloc "of the oppressed" and excluded, and in this the *plebs* can be distinguished from both the entire dominant community as well as from the future community (the *populus*). In the case of Evo Morales the *pueblo*, the "social bloc of the oppressed," comes to be constituted as a "historic bloc in power" (obediential *power*, to judge from its initial actions and declarations at the beginning of 2006).

[11.3.3] Now we can understand that the "popular" is that which is proper to the *people* in the strict sense (referring to the "social bloc of the oppressed") and which represents the last point of reference and regenerative reserve of politics (*hyperpotentia*). This *hyperpotentia* [» 12], however, only exists in itself. The "popular" persists as culture, customs, economics, and ecology underneath all processes, especially when there exist premodern *peoples* (like the Mayas, Aymaras, Quechuas, etc.), which while accompanying Modernity will eventually move beyond it (as part of a transcapitalist, *trans*modern civilization, which is distinct from the still very modern, Eurocentric, and metropolitan understanding of the *post*modern).

[11.3.4] When the *people* gives rise to institutions (*potestas*)—for example, during the approximate period from 1930 to 1954 in Latin America—it can only organize "populist" regimes. I am therefore dealing with the move to a "historical bloc in power" that attempts—in the Latin American cases in question—a limited bourgeois project of emancipation from the metropolitan bourgeoisie or the geopolitical "core" and of social integration through the strengthening of a protected national market (which was possible between the two world wars). The quasi-revolutions of Vargas, Cárdenas, and Perón were the events of the twentieth century that managed to achieve the greatest degree of hegemony, but they remained within the capitalist horizon of a "social pact" with the nascent industrial working class and traditional peasantry. Up to the end of the century, "populism" as a mode of institutionalization had been the most effective in terms of fulfilling "popular" demands. Today, in contrast, Donald Rumsfeld uses the word "populist" as an insult with a meaning along the lines of demagogic, fascistic, and pertaining to the far Right. This careless definition will not persist very long because it has no basis in theory. It is the superficial, rhetorical denigration of an opponent.

LIBERATORY POWER AS *HYPERPOTENTIA* AND
THE "STATE OF REBELLION"

[12.1] THE WILL-TO-LIVE OF THE EXCLUDED:
TOTALITY AND EXTERIORITY

[12.1.1] The victims of the prevailing political system *cannot live* fully (this is why they are victims). Their *Will-to-Live* has been negated by the *Will-to-Power* of the powerful. This *Will-to-Live* against all adversity, pain, and imminent death is transformed into an infinite source for the creation of the new. The will of the singular subjects that comprise movements and the *people* come to acquire an *ethos* of courage, daring, and creativity. The first determination of power (as *potentia* [» 2]) is will, and this is what the *people* recover in conjunctural moments of great transformation.

[12.1.2] The political system, the existing order, finally closes in on itself as a Totality. Emmanuel Levinas, in his work *Totality and Infinity: An Essay on Exteriority*,[83] describes this process of the totalitarian totalization of the Totality "as the exclusion of the Other" (*B* in figure 9), which Marx completes by adding those oppressed by the system (*A* in figure 9). The *people* therefore maintain a complex position. On the one hand, they are the social bloc "of the oppressed" within the system (*A*) (for example, the working class), but they simultaneously comprise the excluded (*B*) (for example, the marginalized, the indigenous peoples who survive through self-sufficient production and consumption, etc.).

[12.1.3] The *conatio vitae conservandi* (life-conserving drive) becomes an extraordinary vital impulse. It tears down the walls of Totality and opens a space

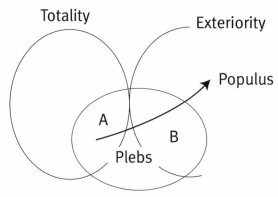

Figure 9. TOTALITY, EXTERIORITY, THE *PEOPLE*

> Notes: Totality, or the prevailing order, fractures. In this way the
> people *are born as the* plebs (*social bloc of the oppressed*), *from
> which Exteriority (due to its unsatisfied demands)—but equally from
> within the Totality (as oppressed)—struggle (exit arrow) toward the
> constitution of the hegemonic* people *of the future (*populus*).*

at the limits of the system through which Exteriority bursts into history.

[12.1.4] Those who are *outside*, like "spectres," ignored, invisible, "do not exist for *political economy* but only for other eyes," as the "man as a mere *workman* who may therefore daily fall from his *filled nothing* into *absolute nothingness*."[84] The *people*, prior to their struggle, are ignored, they do not exist except as *things* at the disposal of the powerful.

[12.1.5] This *conatio*, this will, is the first determination of a moment in the development of the concept of power. Mere *potentia* [» 2] is transformed into something new and distinct that springs from the oppressed, from the excluded, from Exteriority.

[12.2] THE CRITICAL CONSENSUS OF THE NEGATED

[12.2.1] But liberatory power is something more. It requires the unifying force of consensus: "The *people* united will never be defeated!" cried the *people* of Nicaragua. Coercive power is grounded in a political community that, when it was hegemonic, had been unified by consensus. When the oppressed and excluded achieve consciousness of the situation, they become dissidents, and this dissidence leads the hegemonic power to lose its consensus, and without obedience this power becomes fetishized, coercive, repressive. In this way, the movements, sectors, and communities that constitute the *people* gain an increased degree of consciousness of the domination of the prevailing system.

[12.2.2] If ethical validity and political legitimacy are based on the symmetrical participation of the affected toward the accomplishment of agreements by giving reasons, then we already know that said validity and legitimacy cannot be perfect. Neither *perfect* symmetry nor *perfect* participation of all affected parties is possible. Necessarily, given the finitude of the human condition, all legitimacy is relative, imperfect, and fallible. The excluded, in turn, could not by definition have participated in the agreement that excludes them, but they can form a new community within their movement, their sector, their class, or in the *people* more broadly. Feminists gain consciousness of masculinist patriarchy even within and against the prevailing patriarchal culture. Their critical consciousness creates a *critical* consensus within their oppressed community, which now stands opposed to the *dominant* consensus from a position of dissidence. I am referring here to a "crisis of legitimacy" and a "crisis of hegemony"—the moment of chaos that emerges prior to and in anticipation of the creation of a new order.

[12.2.3] This *critical consensus of the people* could not have been discovered either by the first Frankfurt school or by Apel and Habermas. For this reason, these thinkers were unable to link "critical theory" with historical political actors, to which they no longer had access given the disappearance of the Jewish community in the Holocaust and the integration of the working class into the "German miracle." We, on the other hand, must link up with this collective actor called the *people*—this bloc that is born and can disappear depending on the conjuncture—or at the very least with new and vital social movements whose goal is to construct "power from below."

[12.2.4] The *people*, then, gains "consciousness *for-itself.*" It recovers the memory of its moments, its forgotten deeds and those hidden by the history of the victors, as Walter Benjamin teaches us. This is no longer "working-class consciousness," but it does not merely oppose it: it integrates the working class. It is the consciousness of the peasant class, of the indigenous peoples, of feminists, anti-racists, and the marginalized . . . of all those ghosts that wander in the exteriority of the system. It is the consciousness of being a *people*.

[12.3] THE EFFECTIVENESS OF THE WEAK: THE HYPERPOTENTIA OF THE VICTIMS IN A "STATE OF REBELLION"

[12.3.1] We now have (a) the Will-to-Live and (b) the critical consensus of the situation in which these subjects are found, their motives of struggle, and the project of their new order (because "another world is possible"). If to these we add the discovery in the course of struggle itself of (c) the feasibility of liberation—of achieving a new hegemony, of transforming (*Veränderung* in Marx's *Theses on Feuerbach*) the existing political order either partially or radically (and in the latter we could speak of revolution)—we have then formulated the three determinations of the power of the *people*, of *hyperpotentia*.

[12.3.2] If *potentia* [» 2] is a capacity belonging to the political community, which now in a position of dominance has organized *potestas* [» 3] in favor of its interests and against the emergent *people*, then *hyperpotentia* is the power of the *people*, its sovereignty and authority (which Hardt and Negri simply eliminate rather than situating it in its proper place)[85] that emerges in creative moments of history to inaugurate great transformations or radical revolutions. This is Benjamin's messianic "now-time." The enemies of the system (the emergent *people*) are now the friends (the "organic intellectuals") of those who are gambling for their liberation, and their old friends (the family of the Pharaoh in the case of Moses) become their enemies and persecute them. The persecution of the "righteous innocent"—from Hidalgo in Mexico to those whose heads are brutally cut off and displayed in public as a sign of humiliation and punishment—is a theme developed by Levinas in his work *Otherwise than Being: Or Beyond Essence*, in which the political actor responsible for the liberation of the *people* is taken hostage in substitution for the other, for the *people*. These are themes of the politics of liberation that need to be further developed.

[12.3.3] This anti-power in the face of the power of domination, this *hyperpotentia* [» figure 10 (thesis 15)] confronting *potentia*, effectively carries out the transformation of *potestas*, now in service of the *people* (*arrow B*). The effectiveness of the weak is greater than many suppose: Napoleon's armies were defeated by the Spanish *people* in arms, and in 2006 the Iraqi *people* are in the process of defeating the most developed military power in human history. The *people* are invincible . . . or rather, it is necessary to kill all of them when they possess this sort of strategically and tactically consensual and effective *Will-to-Live*. When they exercise the *ethos* of courage!

[12.3.4] Such a situation arises with the phenomenal appearance in the light of day of *hyperpotentia* as a "state of rebellion" (beyond the "government by law" and "state of exception"). Against liberalism's fetishism of the "government by law" (over and above the lives of the excluded), Schmitt proposed the case of the "state of exception" to show the constituent *will* that exists behind the law.[86] Agamben continues this line of argument,[87] and so too we hope to develop it to its ultimate conclusion.

[12.3.5] We need to show how the *people* can suspend the "state of exception" through what I will call the "state of rebellion." In Buenos Aires, the Argentinean *people*, having been swindled by the World Bank and the International Monetary Fund—instruments of Empire and a fetishized national elite—took to the streets en masse on December 20, 2001, to oppose a decree that declared a "state of exception" meant to paralyze the mobilizations. Under the slogan "Que se vayan todos," or "Out with them all!"—in which *hyperpotentia* reminded *potestas* that it remains the last instance of power—the government of Fernando de la Rúa was brought down. That is, the "state of rebellion" disarmed the "state of exception." The will of delegated *auctoritas*—to recall Agamben's distinction—ended up being annulled by a prior will: the will of the *people*, power as *hyperpotentia*.

[12.3.6] The *people*, then, appears as a collective actor—neither substantive nor metaphysical, but conjunctural—as a "bloc" that manifests itself and disappears, in possession of the *new* power that lies below the praxis of anti-hegemonic liberation and the transformation of institutions, the subjects of the next thesis.

13

THE POLITICAL PRINCIPLES OF LIBERATION: THE CRITICAL MATERIAL PRINCIPLE

[13.0.1] In part 1 [» 2–10] I concluded with an explication of the normative principles of politics, because these are *implicit* in all actions and institutions of the political actor whose vocation is to fulfill the demands of obediential power [» 4]. In part 2, which represents the more critical interventions of liberation praxis, the operative principles must be described at the outset, because political actors who create history anew, who introduce innovation into actions and institutions, and who act first on behalf of the excluded, the victims, and the poor, are actors *with principles*—principles that are, moreover, *explicit*. They are conscious of directing their actions and the transformation of political institutions on the basis of the normative demands of those who can reply clearly and with reasons.

[13.0.2] Emiliano Zapata, a political actor from Anenecuilco (which is not far from where I write this), possessed clear principles: (1) "Land for those who work it with their own hands!" (critical material principle); (2) "We always make decisions together, and afterward no one *backs out!*" (critical legitimacy principle); and (3) as a last resort, "We will take up arms!" to defend land against the decisions taken by large landowners (critical feasibility principle). In Zapata's Ayala Plan, point 15, we can read the following: "*We are not personalistic, we are partisans of principles and not of persons!*"[88]

[13.1] CRITICAL POLITICAL PRINCIPLES

[13.1.1] Normative political principles, which subsume critical ethical principles within the political field,[89] constitute political power from within, as the power of the *people, potentia,* and as the exercise of delegated power through institutions, *potestas.* But because like all political *systems* (*level B.6* in table 2 [thesis 10]) this can never be perfect (to be so would require infinite time, intelligence, and will, etc.), and as a result it *inevitably* produces *negative effects* that are in the best of cases unintentional (*level A.12–13* in table 2). That is, negative political effects are a practical mistake, and one can either ignore errors (as do unjust politicians, trapped by their blindness) or recognize and correct them (a characteristic of great politicians). Regardless, there are members of the community who suffer negative political effects on their living corporeality (as pain, humiliation, dissatisfaction, and even death): these are the victims of political injustices, those in oppressed, excluded, marginalized, and exploited classes, those in dominated groups—all those sectors that constitute part of the *people* [» 11.1]. They are victims because they cannot live fully (material moment), because they have been excluded from participating in decisions that harm them (formal moment of illegitimacy), and because they manifest in their own suffering and unsatisfied demands the ineffectiveness of the system (at least with respect to these victimized groups).

[13.1.2] Normative political principles are in the first place *negative*, referring as they do to an unjust positivity. Since it is the prevailing system (the given, the *positive* as Horkheimer puts it) that produces these victims (the *negative*, since they-cannot-live, they-cannot-participate, etc.), the demand or obligation that the political vocation imposes—in starting from a position of solidarity with the humiliated other, which surpasses the mere fraternity of the "we" of the hegemonic community in power—is to refuse and negate the truth, the legitimacy, and the efficacy of that system. The discovery of the *non-truth* (as Adorno wrote), of the *non-legitimacy*, the *non-efficiency* of the system of domination is a moment of skeptical criticism with respect to that system, the moment of atheism toward the prevailing totality, as Marx correctly described it in accordance with prophets of Israel, who rejected the divinity of fetishes.

[13.1.3] The initial formulation of all critical political principles should be the following: *We must criticize, or reject as unsustainable, all political systems, actions, and institutions whose negative effects are suffered by oppressed or excluded victims!*

[13.1.4] We cannot be complicit in a political domination that is the fulfillment of an exercise of power that, instead of serving as an obedient delegate of the *people* [» 4], has become fetishized [» 5].

[13.2] THE MATERIAL PRINCIPLE OF LIBERATION AS A DEMAND FOR THE AFFIRMATION AND ENHANCEMENT OF THE LIFE OF THE COMMUNITY

[13.2.1] Politics, as consensual and feasible Will-to-Live, should attempt through all means to allow all members to live, to live well, and to increase the quality of their lives. In this sense, political normativity appears as an obligation analogous to that of ethics. We are speaking, then, of the material sphere, the *content* of politics. Human life, as the material criterion par excellence, is the ultimate content of all political actions and all institutions. The victim is a victim because he or she *cannot-live*. The politician by vocation is called upon to work in favor of the reproduction and the qualitative improvement of the lives of all citizens. But the victims of the imperfect system, which is inevitably unjust in some moments and intolerably unsustainable during its terminal crises (when injustice multiplies the suffering of the exploited and the excluded), are those who suffer most, like open wounds, the sickness of the social body. They show the *location* of the system's pathology, the injustice that we need to know how to repair.

[13.2.2] The affirmation of the life of the victim, who cannot-live as a result of the injustice of the system, is at the same time that which allows the fulfillment of the demand for improving the life of the community (or of the new institution or system that must be created). I repeat: the mere reproduction of the life of the poor requires such changes that, at the same time, it produces the *civilizing development* of *the entire system*. The affirmation of the life of the victim is at the same time the historical improvement of the entire community. It has been largely through solving the dissatisfaction of the oppressed, the last, that historical systems have progressed.

[13.2.3] The general critical principle, now in its *affirmative* moment, should be expressed as the following: We must produce and reproduce the lives of the oppressed and excluded, the victims, discovering the causes of their negativity and adequately transforming institutions to suit them, which will as a result improve the life of the community as a whole.

[13.2.4] It has often been forgotten that it is the role and obligation of the political actor, as representative, to develop the lives of all citizens, and in the first place those who have been denied the possibility of fulfilling their own needs, from the most basic to the most advanced.

[13.2.5] Politics, in its noblest obediential form, is this responsibility for life, with a special attention to the lives of the poorest, and this fundamental normative demand constitutes the creative moment of politics as liberation. Those communities that have known well enough to give rise to exemplary political leaders have been able to overcome the difficulties that history has had in store! Those with corrupt, egoistic politicians constrained by petty horizons have suffered some bitter moments of defeat, even to the point of disappearing! The fetishization of power by leaders weakens the community and leaves it defenseless against its enemies.

[13.3] THE ECOLOGICAL, ECONOMIC, AND CULTURAL DIMENSIONS OF THE CRITICAL MATERIAL PRINCIPLE OF POLITICS

[13.3.1] The political field traverses [» 7.3, 9.3, 18] the material fields par excellence, which include at the very least the ecological, economic, and cultural fields. These fields determine the *material sphere* of politics, and within each the critical material principle of politics gives rise to particular demands, all of which have to do with the lives of the citizens but operate distinctly in the various dimensions that make up this sphere.

[13.3.2] In the *ecological* subsphere of politics, human life finds itself in direct danger of total extinction. What had never before been foreseeable is today a possibility: from the atomic bomb to the increasing contamination and pollution of planet Earth, the disappearance of life is an imminent prospect. Departing from this absolute limit, we can also see that contamination shortens lives, prevents a sufficient level of health in the population, and generally degrades the conditions for the living corporeality of the citizenry. The material political principle presents itself as an obligation that did not restrict political actors in the same manner that it did in other historical periods, when the Earth was imagined to possess an infinite supply of air, water, and nonrenewable goods. The Earth has shrunk, become finite, and run out of resources. Human beings are responsible for the death of life on our small planet, and this begins to produce a feeling of claustrophobia. The *critical ecological principle of politics* could be expressed as follows: We must behave in all ways such that life on planet Earth might be a *perpetual life!* This, moreover, constitutes a postulate. Nonrenewable goods are holy, irreplaceable, and immensely scarce. We need to go to great lengths to conserve them for future generations. This is perhaps the single most important normative demand of this *new politics*.

[13.3.3] In the *economic* subsphere of politics, the capitalist system has become supremely dangerous, both ecologically and socially. This system— whose only rational basis is the criterion of an increasing profit rate—gives rise to the technological destruction of life on Earth, and it produces as an effect, through the tendency to reduce salaries to a minimum, an immense degree of poverty, unemployment, and misery. The normative *critical-normative* economic principle of politics could be expressed as follows: We must imagine new economic systems and institutions that allow for the reproduction and growth of human life instead of capital! Such alternatives need to be crafted on all institutional levels and with the assistance of the entire *people:* we must train our sights on new popular experiences with alternative social economies.

[13.3.4] In the *cultural* subsphere of politics it is necessary to overcome the Eurocentrism of colonial Modernity through the affirmation of multiculturalism within the population of the national political system. This principle could be put as follows: We must support the cultural *Identity* of all communities included within the political system, and defend cultural *Difference* against efforts to homogenize the cultures and languages of a population through the dominance of some (modern European Creoles or mestizos) and the exclusion of others! We need to embark upon a Cultural Revolution! This is the principle proposed to us from Bolivia by Evo Morales.

THE CRITICAL-DEMOCRATIC AND STRATEGIC
TRANSFORMATION PRINCIPLES

[14.1] THE CRITICAL-DEMOCRATIC PRINCIPLE

[14.1.1] The fulfillment of the normative democratic principle allows for legitimate actions and for the organization of new legitimizing institutions. The prevailing system inevitably produces negative effects, and it becomes slowly transformed—by the entropy of institutions through time—into a coercive fetish. The hegemonic historical bloc has consistently produced victims—namely, groups of the excluded who are constituted in the new social movements, themselves serving as constituent moments of the *people* [» 11]. These communities or movements of the oppressed and excluded become organized and gain consciousness of their oppression, their exclusion, and their unsatisfied needs, and bit by bit they create a *consensus* about their intolerable situation, the cause of their negativity, and the need for struggle. This consensus is a *critical* one that now creates *dissensus* vis-à-vis the old *prevailing* agreement that constituted these same oppressed and excluded groups within the obedient mass subservient to power "as legitimate domination" (in Weber's definition, which was in reality *fetishized power* [» 5], with only *apparent* legitimacy). The consensus of the dominated marks the moment of birth of a *critical democratic* exercise.

[14.1.2] The principle of critical legitimacy or liberatory democracy—which must be completely distinguished from liberal democracy—could be expressed thus: We must achieve a *critical consensus*—first, *through the real and symmetrical participation of the oppressed and excluded*—of the victims of the political system because they are the most affected by the institutional decisions that were made in the past!

[14.1.3] Democracy was always an institutional system, and it is also a normative principle that always seeks to overcome the limits of the previously determined definition of who represented effective members of the community. The excluded always exerted pressure for participation in the creation of consensus—even in the Greek *demos*, seeking to arrive at *isonomia*, or "equal right"—and this struggle for the recognition of their rights required a transformation of the existing democratic system to open it up both to a higher degree of legitimacy and to participation—that is, to democracy. The excluded should not be merely *included* in the *old* system—as this would be to introduce the Other into the Same—but rather ought to participate as equals in a *new institutional moment* (the *new* political order). This is a struggle not for *inclusion* but for *transformation* [» 17], and here I disagree with Iris Young, Habermas, and countless others who speak so often of "inclusion."

[14.1.4] Because the *people* are the principal actors, critical, liberatory, or popular democracy calls into question the previous degree of achieved democratization, since democracy is a system to be perennially reinvented.

[14.1.5] I should make clear, since there exists great confusion on this point, that *critical* democracy—which is social but equally includes the material sphere as well as ecological, economic, and cultural conflicts that produce the crisis embodied in "the social problem"—is on the one hand a *normative principle*, an obligation of the political vocation, the militant, and the citizen in favor of the *people*, but it is also an *institutional system* that one needs to know how to transform permanently. It is in innovation—the institutional creativity of overcoming the fetishized moments that did not respond to the reality of the democrat—that the real possibility for political development lies, a development that is never interrupted and moreover *never* reaches perfection. I am speaking again of a postulate: "We must struggle for an always increasingly democratic system!" whose *perfect* empirical institutionalization is impossible.

[14.2] THE PRINCIPLE OF STRATEGIC LIBERATION

[14.2.1] Feasibility, then, is the final link in the chain, as I have shown repeatedly. This is because once the life of the victim (ecological, economic, cultural) has been affirmed and has managed to organize itself to arrive at a critical democratic consensus, the issue is to bring into practice, into historical reality, the effective institutionalization of the political *project* that has been germinating. This is where the political actor by vocation—the critical politician or the participatory citizen—encounter many pitfalls and difficulties to be avoided. The actions and institutions that are to be actualized must also be *possible*. As opposed to the politics of a prevailing system—with its traditions, tendencies, and established institutions—those who transform an existing and unjust system are confronted with much more difficult strategic decisions. Machiavelli did not pen his brief treatise, *Il Principe*, for a traditional politician exercising power but rather for a *new* governor who hopes to begin a *new* political era. In this case, the *possibility* of making one's objectives a reality is a much more difficult prospect—that is, it has a lesser degree of feasibility. Now, its *possibility* can be situated more clearly between that which the anarchist believes to be empirically *possible* (but which is merely a postulate [» 17.3]), and that which the conservative of the existing order believes to be *impossible*. That which is *possible* for the critical and liberatory political actor, one who is accountable to the victims of the system, falls short of anarchist possibility (which is really impossible) and surpasses conservative *im*possibility (possible only if the prevailing conditions of oppression and exclusion are transformed).

[14.2.2] The critical feasibility principle in politics could be formulated as follows: We must do the maximum *possible*—thereby appearing reformist to the anarchist [» 17.2] and suicidal to the conservative—and having as criterion of possibility in institutional creation (transformation) the liberation of the victims of the current system, the *people!* Only triumphant social movements or an exceptional political leader—who in reality proceeds by assessing the transformative capacity or *hyperpotentia* [» 12] of the *people* itself—know what is feasible or infeasible or how to stretch the rope of transformation to the *maximum* without breaking it.

[14.2.3] Given that the critical political actor confronts the entire established institutionality of the old regime—the historic bloc exercising fetishized power—the struggle of the *people* for its liberation (partial or radical [» 17.2]) needs to be much more strategic and intelligent than the dominators. An error of calculation could break a cat's claw, but it could cost the mouse its life.

[14.2.4] The critical normative political principle promotes creativity, fraternity, and the emergence of the *hyperpotentia* of the *people* [» 12]. A *people* whose mind is made up, and who thereby exist in a "state of rebellion," can be defeated neither definitively nor militarily, as Clausewitz commented on observing Napoleon's disastrous Spanish campaign, a situation repeated by the United States in Vietnam and, today, in Iraq.

[14.3] THE NOBLE VOCATION OF POLITICS

[14.3.1] Simply because a politician exercises obediential power does not mean that he or she is immune to making mistakes. Indeed, a Semitic saying reminds us that "a just person commits seven sins a day," and a popular saying teaches us that "to err is human, to pardon is divine." One might ask, How many sins does it take to make one unjust? The answer is none, because the unjust person is precisely one who never takes conscious responsibility for the negative effects of his or her actions. As the unjust person always carries out corrupt actions and attempts to hide these, he or she cannot differentiate inevitable (and unintentional) negative effects from whose that are willingly corrupt. All acts become suspect. In this attempt to avoid the blame for all of the negative effects of one's acts we find instead injustice and corruption. As a result, the honest politician cannot be *perfectly* just. Perfection is only proper to gods, and it is impossible for the human condition. Given this impossibility for extreme perfection, what is demanded normatively of the politician by vocation is that he or she honestly fulfills in the most serious manner possible the conditions for a just act. This is what can be deemed the "political justice claim."

[14.3.2] In other words the political actor, like all finite human beings, cannot be deemed bad for having committed political mistakes. Human finitude cannot avoid erroneous acts but instead can only attempt seriously and with good will to fulfill the conditions for being just. Those who honestly attempt to fulfill these conditions can be said to possess the justice "claim." To be precise, this word "claim" indicates that those engaging in an action can justify it by giving reasons and by showing that the action is an attempt to affirm life feasibly and through the consensus of those affected. The three critical principles laid out above are the conditions for this "political justice claim."

[14.3.3] But there is more: these stated normative principles are also what allow us to determine when someone commits political mistakes (through not fulfilling one of these), and, moreover, the way to correct those mistakes depends on the same three critical principles (the material, the formal, and the feasible). These critical normative principles are, then, principles that constitute and illuminate liberatory actions and the transformation of institutions, which allow us to discover mistakes and, finally, which function as criteria for the correction of the injustices committed. Without principles, the political actor who attempts to adopt a critical stance finds himself or herself in the position of the ship captain caught in the middle of a storm without a compass: that is, lost!

[14.3.4] On the other hand, those with access to critical normative principles—which never negate but rather only subsume the procedural creativity of actions, institutions, administration, etc.—find themselves able to confront profound crises, devastating political struggles, and even handle contempt, partial defeat, and patient work on long-range projects. This extends, finally, to the limit cases involving death itself—as with Miguel Hidalgo y Costilla— since those who know how to face death incorruptibly are only feared by oppressors. This represents the *maximum* possible degree of feasibility, when the very life of the *people* is offered in order to save itself. Heroes necessarily confront unforeseeable events, but they always improve upon each action by remaining inspired by clear and effective critical normative political principles.

[14.3.5] When the political actor exercises *obediential* power through delegation, when he or she has an honest critical-political aspiration toward justice, we can say that he or she fulfills the noble vocation of politics. To serve the *people* through militant obedience produces in the subjectivity of the citizen and the politician a sort of joy similar to that of Marx when, as an eighteen-year-old student, he wrote the following: "But the chief guide which must direct us in the choice of a profession is the welfare of mankind . . . History calls those men the greatest who have *ennobled* themselves by working for the common good; experience acclaims as happiest the man who has made the greatest number of *people* happy; religion itself teaches us that the ideal being whom all strive to copy sacrificed himself for the sake of mankind."[90] This exemplary universalistic, public, and humanistic normative-political ideal is clearly a far cry from the political egoism and privatizing individualism of liberalism and from the competitive economic avarice of capitalism.

LIBERATION PRAXIS OF SOCIAL AND POLITICAL MOVEMENTS

15

[15.0.1] *Praxis* indicates the actuality of the subject in the world, and political *praxis* implies its presence in the political field. But a praxis of *liberation* (*arrows A* and *B* in figure 10) calls into question the hegemonic structures of the political system (*potestas 1*). Institutional *transformations* (*arrow B*) partially or totally change the structure of mediations in the delegated exercise of power (from *potestas 1* we move to *potestas 2*).

[15.0.2] Political action intervenes in the political field, always modifying the given structure of the political field in some way. All subjects, upon becoming actors—and especially when representing a movement or *people*—become the motor, the force, the power that *makes history*. When this is a "practical-critical activity,"[91] I will refer to it as *liberation praxis* (*Befreiungspraxis* in Marx and Horkheimer). This praxis has two moments: a *negative* struggle, deconstructive of the given (*arrow A* in figure 10), and a *positive* moment of outlet, of the construction of the new (*arrow B*). Insofar as this "liberates"—as in the act by which the slave is emancipated from slavery—its creative potential is opposed to and finally triumphs over the structures of domination, exploitation, and exclusion that weigh heavily upon the *people*. The power of the *people—hyperpotentia*, the new power of those "from below"—becomes present from the beginning, in its extreme vulnerability and poverty, but is in the end the invincible

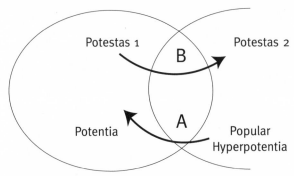

Figure 10. LIBERATION PRAXIS AND INSTITUTIONAL TRANSFORMATION

force of life "that desires-to-live." This Will-to-Live is more powerful than death, injustice, and corruption.

[15.1] UTOPIAS AND PARADIGM: POSSIBLE MODELS, PROJECTS, STRATEGIES, TACTICS, MEANS

[15.1.1] "During years and years we harvested the death of our own *people* in the fields of Chiapas. . . . Our steps moved forward with no destination, we only lived and died."[92] But one day the *people*, their movements and the leadership that obeys them, awaken, stand up, and say "Enough!" They enter into history through their *liberatory praxis*. This action has a logic, a demand, and it is guided especially by the critical political principle of feasibility, since what is *possible* confronts various apparent practical impossibilities that need to be overturned. The praxis of liberation demands principles, coherence, resoluteness to the death, and infinite patience (like that of our original *peoples* during the past five hundred years, from confrontations with Cortés, Pizarro, and Almagro to the triumph of Evo Morales).

[15.1.2] Rosa Luxemburg has a lovely text that deals with strategy against those "reformists" who have no "principles" (or "theory")[93]: "The principles of scientific socialism, impose clearly *marked limitations* [*feste Schränke*] to practical activity, insofar as it concerns the *aims* of this activity, the *means* used in attaining these aims and the *method* employed in this activity. It is quite natural for *people* who run after immediate 'practical' results to want to *free* themselves from such limitations and to render their practice independent of our '*theory*' [read: *principles*]."[94]

[15.1.3] We therefore need to keep various levels in mind during critical, anti-hegemonic praxis, which develops out of many prior moments and confronts the "historical bloc in power": *level A.ıı* in table 2 (thesis 10).

[15.1.4] First there is the most distant horizon, which we could refer to as Utopian, in which we descriptively imagine a state of affairs. Such a horizon is more accurately understood as a *political postulate* [» 17.3] such as those of the World Social Forum that state, "Another world is possible!" or "A world in which many worlds fit!" Such postulates might seem too empty, but they are the condition of possibility for all the rest, since without the *hope* for a world that we need to make possible—so closely studied by Ernst Bloch[95]—there cannot exist a critical, liberation praxis. It is necessary to creatively imagine the notion "Yes we can!" in order to be able to change things. In other words, we need to always keep *potestas 2*—the *future* institutional structure that will be at the service of the *people*, and which indicates this Utopian pole—affirmatively in our minds. This is *level C.4–5* in table 2.

[15.1.5] Second, in political practice or theory we must progressively sketch a *paradigm or model of possible transformation*, which is not simple and often shifts throughout time, such that it cannot always be delineated in a detailed fashion. Against liberal democracy, the welfare State, or Keynesian economics (structures that are located in various fields), and against the transitional democracies of Latin America (since 1983) that generate a frequently corrupt "political class," we must move forward with the formulation of a *new* "paradigm" or "model." Such a model would entail broad participation, popular hegemony, national identity (especially in postcolonial or peripheral countries), the defense of the economic interests of the weakest (impossible to fulfill through neoliberal capitalism and its globalizing strategy of the domination and exploitation of subaltern nations), and a renewed administrative effectiveness grounded in a new "social pact" and, moreover, in new constitutions that give rise to new structures within a transformed State.

[15.1.6] Third, on an even more concrete level, we need to work toward a *project for feasible transformations* (*level A.7* in table 2), in which the *concrete* goals of liberatory action in all spheres (material, legitimacy, State administration) are made explicit. These would be properly political but simultaneously critical, and they would operate by way of *critical*, liberatory, and progressive political parties [» 15.3], as well as through teams of scientists (political scientists, economists, educators, doctors, union leaders, representatives of social movements, etc.). This project could be expressed in the short term through criteria and concrete theses for efficient feasible realization within a government cycle (of four to six years), but it must also be accompanied by medium-term (about twenty-five years) and *long-term* projects for popular participation (especially with regard to ecological and transcapitalist economic questions).

[15.1.7] Fourth, political leaders need to have *strategic* clarity (*level A.8* in table 2) in their transformative action. On this level, projects need to be administratively and conjuncturally implemented with an eye to the transformation of institutions. This level depends on the practical wisdom (*prudence*) of political actors operating within a democratic system to produce consensual decisions, in a team, through participation "from below" (from popular movements, the *people*, neighborhoods, rural communities, etc.). This strategy should be elaborated democratically and as a whole on all levels.

[15.1.8] Fifth, it is necessary to formulate *efficient tactics* (*level A.9* in table 2), which constitute mediations for carrying out the strategies that have been elaborated theoretically, in the practice of forming cadres, in the election of candidates as representatives, in propaganda itself, in the ideological and normative orientation of said informational process, in the mode of action, etc.

[15.1.9] Sixth, *appropriate means* must be selected for all of the aspects mentioned above (*level A.10* in table 2), but only among those that are *possible* given the demands that structure all of the described levels (fulfilling principles, postulates, models, etc.). A purely *Machiavellian* tactical approach (one not ascribed to by Machiavelli) in which "the ends justify any means" is always destructive in the end, both for the actor as well as for the *people*. This is because feasible means—and here Horkheimer's *Critique of Instrumental Reason* is worth considering—that appear to be more efficient may end up losing sight of the "principles" (as Luxemburg tells us). As a result, one loses the "clearly marked limitations" that create coherence, positive effects in the long run, and clarity of action, thanks to which *confidence* in the *people* is mutually crafted. As Fidel Castro puts it, "When the *people* believe in the *people*," that is, the point at which the political actor and the citizen awaken this faith from "the top down" (as *obediential* power) and from "the bottom up" (as faith in honest, principled action, which is the condition of just, normative, and effective leadership of the *delegated* power of the governor). Machiavelli demanded a certain *virtù* by which politicians construct "dikes" to constrain the impetuous and destructive force of *Fortuna*, the chaotic and unforeseeable events of everyday politics that need to be resolved in the same manner but without losing sight of serving the *people* as the obediential exercise of power.

[15.2] ORGANIZATION OF NEW SOCIAL MOVEMENTS AND STRUGGLES OVER DEMANDS

[15.2.1] Liberation praxis is not solipsistic—that is, it is not created by a single and inspired subject: the leader (who should necessarily be distinguished from *obediential* leadership). Liberation praxis is *always* an intersubjective community act of reciprocal consensus, which does not reject leadership, as we have said, but definitively abandons vanguardism. It is a "rearguard" action by the *people* itself, which educates social movements about its democratic autonomy, its political evolution, and about being mutually responsible for its destiny. The liberation politician, Gramsci's organic intellectual, is more a promoter, an organizer, and a light that illuminates the path constructed, unfolded, and perfected by the *people*. Political leadership is service, obedience, coherence, intelligence, discipline, and devotion.

[15.2.2] To fulfill the Will-to-Live, popular movements and the *people* need to be organized, and this organization already represents a passage from *potentia* (the power of the *people*, of social movements) to *potestas* (that power which is granted institutions for them to concretely exercise delegated power). Without this separation, without this split (between potential power *in-itself* and institutional power *for-itself*), and without organization, the power of the *people* remains pure *potential*, possibility, objective nonexistence, ideal voluntarism, and anarchism. To organize a movement, a *people*, is to create heterogeneous and differentiated functions, in which each member learns to fulfill different responsibilities but all within the consensual unity of the *people*. This is an intermediary, social, civil level of the delegated exercise of power, a political institutionalization of Civil Society, within the State in the broad, Gramscian sense. Through organization, the homogeneous, undifferentiated, and thereby impotent community—consensual wills that nevertheless lack feasibility, since feasibility is functional and differential concretization—achieves the possibility of exercising power. It becomes *potent*: "able-to-create" the means for its own survival [» 2.1].[96]

[15.2.3] In order to hunt during the paleolithic era, humans needed to be organized: one person preparing the weapons, another scouting the area, another gives the attack cry, another advances on the right flank, another on the left, still another seizes the prey, another distributes it, and as a result all needs are satisfied: in short, they live. In order to improve life—in ecological, economic, cultural, and religious terms, etc.—the differentiation of functions, or organization, is essential. Today this organization must be *democratic*, always and in all its instances, with the *symmetrical* participation of all those affected by domination and exclusion. Luxemburg anticipated the collapse of actually existing socialism based precisely upon difficulties on the organizational level: "We can conceive of no greater danger to the Russian party than Lenin's plan of organization. *Nothing will more surely enslave a young labor movement to an intellectual elite hungry for power than this bureaucratic straitjacket, which will immobilize the movement and turn it into an automaton manipulated by a Central Committee.* . . . The game of bourgeois demagogues will be made easier if at the present stage, the spontaneous action, initiative, and political sense of the advanced sections of the working class are hindered in their development and restricted by the protectorate of an authoritarian Central Committee."[97]

[15.2.4] Even in the Sandinista movement there was a tendency to "send down" orders from above to the Sandinista masses. Only with Zapatismo has vanguardism been definitively overcome. Democracy is not a slogan but rather a necessary moment in the subjectivity of the political actor, an institution to be practiced on all levels of the organization of popular movements, within movements, among different movements, and as a demand put forward to progressive, critical, and liberatory political parties.

[15.3] THE ORGANIZATION OF PROGRESSIVE POLITICAL PARTIES

[15.3.1] Progressive, critical, liberatory political parties should function like the mythical Mayan "tree of life" that sinks its roots into *terra mater* (the *people*), raises its trunk over the terrestrial surface (Civil Society), and unfolds its foliage and fruits in the sky (in Political Society, the State in the restricted sense). The party, therefore, is the *location* where the representative can regenerate his or her *delegation* of power *constructed from below*. The member base of the party must be able to demand explanation, to reprimand, and to criticize its partner-in-faith, the representative, when these individuals betray their principles or fail to fulfill their promises. The party is where political theory is discussed and produced, where utopias are sketched, and where concrete projects and the strategies to achieve proposed goals and other levels of liberation praxis are formulated. It is where candidates for elections are decided upon democratically. It is where a well-thought-out, discussed, and grounded opinion of a type of future society, a concrete model, is developed, bearing in mind the historical development of the political, geopolitical, national, and global present.

[15.3.2] Unfortunately, the Latin American political parties that have existed since the installation of transitional democracies in 1983 have fetishized the "political class" that exercises power monopolistically. These parties are in need of profound transformation, as they are often little more than *electoral machines*, which like antediluvian fossils begin to move when they make out on the horizon an election for *paid* functionaries. The temptation for payment, the perverse pleasure of the fetishized exercise of power, plunges groups, sectors, and internal movements into proportional distribution (in proportion to their corruption, clearly), to get carried away with possible candidacies in the face of the scandalous and very public presence of the *people*, which they claim to represent and serve. The party as *electoral machine* is rotten—it is useless for the critique, transformation, or liberation demanded by popular movements; useless for the oppressed and excluded *people*. It is a scandal! To democratize a party and impede the subsidies to which it feels entitled as the representative of the monopolistic "political class" means to universalize its cadres, to dissolve its internal divisions, and to allow the movement of opinion in theoretical discussions, projects, and concrete proposals (but not only nor even principally in the election of candidates). Perhaps a Party Youth contingent, not summoned by internal groupings but rather by the party as a whole, might be able in the medium term to provide a bodily spirit to those parties that arise from particularistic, personalistic, corporative, and local strongman alliances, and that lack an ideology sufficient for the demands of the *people*, and especially the poor. Party corruption results from a loss of ideological clarity regarding the paradigm being struggled for, the nonexistence of research and discussion projects, and a lack of ethical coherence among party cadres.

[15.3.3] Parties must be regenerated through both subjective and objective-ideological discipline, thanks to which the daily conduct of the politician might relate more coherently to party principles. To do so would mean to operate according to a shared responsibility toward the exploited and the poor, with the goal of creating conditions of respect for symmetry in democratic participation, with the compromise of those who roll up their sleeves, take off their shoes, and get dirty, getting blistered hands . . . alongside the *people*. We need a new generation of politicians, perhaps a younger one, who will enthusiastically assume the noble vocation of politics!

[15.3.4] Party organization must reflect the demands of the times in impoverished peripheral countries. The winds that arrive from the South—from Nestor Kirchner, Tabaré Vásquez, Luiz Inácio Lula da Silva, Evo Morales, Hugo Chávez, Fidel Castro, and so many others—show us that things can be changed. The *people* must reclaim sovereignty! The elections of popular leaders and candidates, the renewed production of foundational documents, projects for educative, industrial, and ecological policies, and concrete proposals—these all must be the fruit of democratic procedures with a symmetrical horizontalism involving the participation of all members, and especially the representation within political parties of neighborhood communities, base committees, and open popular councils, in which direct democracy teaches the humble citizen how to truly participate in popular politics. This participation should then be equally organized "upward" to constitute Citizen Power, as the supreme Power controlling all other State Powers [» 19.34, 20.23].

[15.3.5] Michael Walzer, in his work *Exodus and Revolution*, writes the following: "First, that wherever you live, it is probably Egypt; second, that there is a better place, a world more attractive, a promised land; and third, that 'the way to the land is through the wilderness.' There is no way to get from here to there except by joining together and marching."[98]

[15.3.6] *Egypt* represents the totality of the prevailing coercive system, the *promised land* is a liberated future, and the *wilderness* is the winding and uncertain path of political strategy: tough, exhausting, full of danger . . . but we must maintain our compass so as not to wander off course and to arrive at the oasis where "milk and honey flow," as the Sandinista hymn goes.

16 ANTI-HEGEMONIC PRAXIS AND THE CONSTRUCTION OF A NEW HEGEMONY

[16.1] HEGEMONIC CRISIS

[16.1.1] The existing empirical institutional political system exercises power hegemonically when the political community accepts it with a sufficient consensus, which means that the demands of various social sectors have been satisfied. But when this situation enters into a crisis when the interests of the oppressed and excluded are not fulfilled, members of this group become conscious of their dissatisfaction and suffering, which upon becoming intolerable—and intolerability is *relative* to understanding the degree of satisfaction achieved by other social groups—produce the irruption of a collective critical consciousness [» 19.2] that then breaks the existing consensus and appears as social dissensus. The hegemony of the "leading class," as Gramsci puts it, becomes "coercive," and this represents a crisis of hegemony—a crisis of the legitimacy of the prevailing political system.

[16.1.2] The praxis of liberation is critical during its initial, anti-hegemonic phase. It ruptures the hegemony of the class in power. It is a praxis whose effectiveness increases in proportion to the decreasing hegemonic legitimacy of the system. There is, then, an increase on the one hand—in the praxis of liberation—and a decrease on the other, as consensual legitimacy gives way to greater domination against a simultaneously increasing dissensus, which like a spiral support one another: the greater the repression and violence, the higher the degree of consciousness and eagerness to work toward freedom. This praxis reveals the "feet of clay" of the existing institutions.[99] The system can have massive armies, intelligence services, and perfectly organized police, but the repressive apparatus (the armor-plated body of the statue), as the expression of a despotic exercise of power (a fetishized *potestas*), ceases to have "strength." It loses its "support" from the power of the *people* below (the *potentia*), and as a result it falls to pieces from its own contradictions in the face of infinitely inferior forces (from an instrumental and quantitative perspective, but not in terms of effective, qualitative power).

[16.1.3] Social movements, as well as liberatory, critical, progressive parties, must be able to learn how to operate from a position of inferior force (in physical, mechanical, coercive terms), relying on the power that surges up "from below," from the *people*.

[16.1.4] It is essential that liberation praxis sets out from the *people*, thereby remaining in its element, and mobilizing from within and from below the collective historical actor that is the *people* (as the *plebs* who will constitute a future *populus*).

[16.1.5] Only Gramsci has been able to describe adequately how the class in power, when confronted with the destruction of consensus by popular dissensus, moves from hegemonic to coercive. As a result, this class exercises power as domination, repression, violence, and even State terrorism in extreme cases (as in the Latin American military dictatorships imposed by the Pentagon from the 1960s to the 1980s, for example).

[16.2] LEGITIMATE COMPULSION, VIOLENCE, AND LIBERATION PRAXIS

[16.2.1] Frequently today we hear talk of terrorism, violence, and "just war," which is not sufficiently distinguished from the justified compulsion of heroic figures like Miguel Hidalgo or George Washington. We need to use different terms in order to discuss actions that have very different normative meanings but are often confused.

[16.2.2] We will use the term *compulsion* to refer to all use of force that is grounded in the "government by law" [» 8.2]. In this definition, Political Society has a monopoly on the legal use of compulsion, since the citizens have

Table 4. LEGITIMATE COMPULSION AND VIOLENCE

	(a) Established (legal) order	*(b) Transformation of the order*
1. Legitimate compulsion	Legal and legitimate actions (A)	Liberation praxis, illegal but legitimate (B)
2. Violence, the use of illegitimate compulsion	Legal but illegitimate repression (C)	Illegal and illegitimate anarchist action (D)

Notes: I distinguish between "legitimacy" and "illegitimacy" in (A) and (B). (A) refers to the current empirical system, which has moved from hegemonic to coercive. In (B) the reference point is a new legitimacy that is established through the critical-transformative or liberatory action of the people. The Laws of the Indies that established the colonial regime of New Spain is represented by legitimacy (A). The new order that Hidalgo sought to establish, which decreed a Constitution in Chilpancingo, is legitimacy (B). Liberation praxis is only "illegal" with respect to the prevailing legal system, which is now repressive. Actions are "legitimate" with respect to the critical consensus of the social movement or political actor. The violent compulsion of the existing order is "legal" in reference to the prevailing system but "illegitimate" with regard to the critical consensus of the oppressed who have gained consciousness of their new rights.

passed the laws and impose obedience upon themselves, thereby in reality obeying themselves (situation *A* in table 4).

[16.2.3] This situation becomes complicated when social movements or the *people* discover *new* rights and struggle for their recognition [» 19.2], and for the oppressed or excluded community these rights create a *new* legitimacy (this is *legitimacy B* in table 4). In this moment, legitimate compulsion (in *1.a*) within the *old* legal system (e.g., Spain's *Laws of the Indies*), becomes illegitimate for those opposed to that system (e.g., the patriots led by Hidalgo) and now appears to them as *violence* (situation *2.a:* C). Action that is purely *violent* (in *2.b:* D), on the other hand, is that which does not involve an entire *people* struggling for its demands, but which instead is composed of a self-appointed anti-institutional vanguard, which does not rely on the consensual, collective, and critical support of the new system of legitimacy (B). *Violence* is also the use of force against the right of another—whether justifiable and legitimate institutions or the actor involved in liberation praxis—and this is always a crime. Hidalgo, when he used even armed force—illegal for the *Laws of the Indies* but legitimate from the point of view of the popular patriotic community, (B)—did not exercise violence but rather legitimate, liberatory compulsion.

[16.2.4] The death of the attacking enemy in a defensive patriotic struggle is justifiable by political normativity and does not stand in opposition to the material principle of life [» 9 and 13], since on a higher and more concrete level of complexity, in which principles conflict with one another, it is necessary to discern priorities: the principle of the defense of the innocent life of the popular community has priority over the life of the invader, who is guilty of aggression and colonialism, etc. In a battle, both armies have different normative qualifications: the American army is an unjustifiable invader of Iraq, and its violence is illegitimate terrorism. The defense of the Iraqi population (or the patriots in Palestine) is defensive, heroic, justifiable: it is legitimate compulsion.

[16.2.5] Clearly I am speaking of limit cases, but these can help us to clarify the concrete application of our principles, rather than falling into a facile acceptance of the conceptual chaos created by the current imperial and economic-military powers.

[16.3] CONSTRUCTION OF A NEW HEGEMONY

[16.3.1] Popular movements, the *people*, need to "construct power from below," as is frequently said in the meetings in Porto Alegre. The power of the *people*— as critical *hyperpotentia*—is constructed "below" (and not merely "from" below), and has as its center the *people* itself. What is "constructed" (not *taken*) is the accumulation of strength, unity, the institutions and subjective normativity of the agents, and only afterward comes the delegated exercise of power (*potestas*). In effect, liberation praxis is *this very* "construction," as it is the action of subjects who have become the *actors* who build the new structure of politics on the basis of a new political "culture."

[16.3.2] Having begun as an anti-hegemonic struggle by the coca farmers' union, when Evo Morales was elected president of Bolivia in December 2005, the transformation of the State began as a praxis of "constructing" hegemony. From the critical opposition—always somewhat *destructive*, dangerous, and negative—we now move to the *positive* exercise of delegated power. The purely negative liberation praxis of the slaves in Egypt (which Tupac Amaru often mentioned during the Andean rebellion) arrives at the River Jordan at the end of the desert. After Moses the liberator dies, and Joshua the ambiguous *constructor* of the *new* order begins to exercise delegated power,[100] this process becomes a praxis that needs a hegemonic project based on the majority (which also includes the best of the *old* regime, because one cannot govern in the minority, despotically and anti-democratically). Liberation praxis becomes creative, imaginative, and innovative of the new order, the fruit of the transformation, which it now needs to be able to administer effectively. This task is much more difficult, complicated, and concrete than mere opposition: it is a responsibility of feasible governance.

[16.3.3] Social movements and progressive, critical political parties must devote themselves to the task of "translating" the demands of all sectors, their differential identities. Through mutual understanding, dialogue, and the inclusion of other demands in their own, this allows them to move forward with the construction of an *analogical hegemon* supported by all, which is transformed into a new proposal as a result of the praxis of popular liberation. The postulate? "A world in which all worlds fit!"

TRANSFORMATION OF POLITICAL INSTITUTIONS: REFORM, TRANSFORMATION, REVOLUTION: POLITICAL POSTULATES

[17.0.1] Institutional transformations (*arrow B* in figure 10 [thesis 15]) change the structure of *potestas 1* (the prevailing political State, as Civil or Political Society) and create either a new institution or (through revolutionary change) a new system: *potestas 2*. Transformation is institutional creation, not merely "taking power." Power is not *taken* but is instead exercised through delegation, and if one wants such delegation to take the form of *obedience* then it is necessary to *transform* many institutional moments (notably, partial or total transformations of the system, not reforms).

[17.0.2] Political philosophy proposes neither concrete empirical projects nor transformations. This task falls to groups of social scientists, political parties, and social movements, on the economic and ecological levels, in education and health care, etc. Here we can only hope to explain principles, the fundamental criteria for transformation in the medium term (fifty years, for example), that will see the overcoming of the old authoritarian or totalitarian Latin American model as well as the recent neoliberal model applied during the last decades of the twentieth century. These will be replaced by a new paradigm that eliminates the monopoly of the "political class" (of bureaucratized parties) that has characterized the period of formal democracy in debtor nations (since 1983 on our political continent).

[17.1.1] Institutions are necessary for the material reproduction of life, for the possibility of legitimate democratic action, and for the achievement of instrumental, technical, and administrative effectiveness [» 7.2]. That they are *necessary* does not mean that they are eternal, perennial, or not transformable. To the contrary, all institutions that are born out of demands specific to a determinate political time, that structure bureaucratic or administrative functions, and that define means and ends are inevitably gnawed upon and eroded by the passing of time: they suffer a process of entropy. At their origin is that disciplinary, creative moment of responding to new demands. In their classic moment, institutions effectively carry out their assignment. But they slowly weaken and enter into crisis: the strength necessary to maintain them becomes greater than their benefits and the bureaucracy they initially created becomes self-referential, defending its own interests over those of the citizens they claim to serve. An institution created for the sake of life begins to operate as an occasion for coercion, exclusion, and even death, and as a result it becomes time to modify it, improve it, abolish it, or replace it with another institution made necessary by the changing times.

[17.1.2] All institutions, all institutional systems, will need to be transformed in the short, medium, or long term. There is no such thing as an everlasting institutional arrangement. The only question is when an institution should continue to operate, when a partial, superficial, or profound transformation is necessary, or simply when a total modification of the particular institution or the entire institutional system must occur.

[17.1.3] The political actor cannot cling to institutions, despite having created them—often with tremendous benefits. Neither should an actor change institutions to suit a passing fad, the desire for novelty, or the hope of leaving "great works" as a testament to his or her time in power.

[17.1.4] Life, in its evolutionary process, produced genetic transformations that allowed for the appearance of new species more adapted to conditions on planet Earth. In the same manner, political life subsumes institutions that have existed for millennia: royal, presidential, and military leadership, the constitution of discursive assemblies comprised of voting members whose legislation is binding and with the means of enforcement, among whom are judges, etc. These are continually actualized and constitute a history of political systems and institutions, which with the support of great technological discoveries— like writing, paper, printing, radio, television, computers, and the Internet, etc.—are capable of surpassing the efficiency of the delegation of popular power in earlier periods.

[17.1.5] If we accept the hypothesis of the Russian economist Kondatrieff of the existence of economic cycles, the last cycle—beginning around 1940 and rooted in the development of the automobile and petroleum—would have become exhausted by the mid-1990s. A new cycle has thus begun its ascendency—with the technological revolution in satellite communications linked with informatics, which allows each citizen to use a computer and connect to global networks—and it should last approximately until 2020. The transformations accomplished during this propitious cycle have a greater potential for stabilization than those carried out, in however revolutionary a manner, during the downswing of the prior cycle (1973–1995).

[17.2] REFORM, TRANSFORMATION, REVOLUTION

[17.2.1] In thinking of Rosa Luxemburg's excellent book *Reform or Revolution* we would be inclined to think that these concepts stand in opposition to one another, but in reality the question is more complex. The real opposition is to be found, as illustrated in figure 11, between "reform" (A) and "transformation" (B), with revolution (B.b) as a radical form of the latter. This question is of the greatest strategic importance.

[17.2.2] In effect, some groups on the left would have us believe that those who do not affirm the empirical and immediate possibility for a revolution are reformists. What occurs in reality is that revolutionary processes of human history can progress for centuries without appearing as visible. It is true that one can prepare for and advance the revolution, but only within the limits of determined time. To think that Latin America finds itself today in a revolutionary conjuncture—as was the case around the time of the Cuban Revolution—is to politically confuse things, producing lamentable mistakes (in fact,

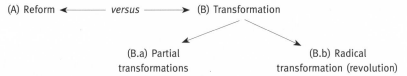

Figure 11. REFORM, TRANSFORMATION, AND REVOLUTION

the failures of the revolution in Chile of Allende, or of Sandinismo in Nicaragua, for example, were due precisely to broader geopolitical shifts).

[17.2.3] Marx's writings should be considered in this respect: "The coincidence of the changing of circumstances and of human activity can be conceived and rationally understood only as *transformative praxis* [*umwälzende Praxis*]. . . . The philosophers have only *interpreted* the world in various ways; the point, however, is to *transform* [*verändern*] it."[101]

[17.2.4] Within twentieth-century leftist tradition, it was understood that if an activity was not "revolutionary" then it was "reformist." If the situation was not objectively revolutionary, then, it became necessary to create—through a certain degree of voluntarism—the conditions through which it would acquire its revolutionary physiognomy. This was political idealism masquerading under the name of revolution, which occasionally produced an extreme political commitment among young people who irresponsibly sacrificed their lives.

[17.2.5] Alternatively, revolutionaries are often believed to use violent means, producing the transformation from one political-economic system to another immediately, through a leap in time. Social democracy, on the other hand, is presented as an opposing, reformist,[102] peaceful, institutionalist approach, etc.

[17.2.6] It is time to radically rethink the question. I will use the term "reformist" to refer only to that action that pretends to change something but in which the institution and the system remain fundamentally the same as before. In this case, the totality of the institutional system receives nothing more than an accidental improvement without responding to new popular demands.

[17.2.7] Political "transformation" means, on the other hand, a change in the form of the innovation of an institution or the radical transmutation of the political system in response to new interventions by the oppressed or excluded. Transformation is carried out, however partially, with reference to the horizon of a *new* way of exercising delegated power (*potestas* 2). Institutions change form (*trans-form*) when there exists a different project that renovates the power of the *people*. In the case of a *transformation* of the *entire institutional system*—the bourgeois English Revolution of the seventeenth century, the socialist revolution in China in the mid-twentieth century, or the 1959 Cuban Revolution—we can speak of revolution, which is always possible a priori (since no system is perpetual) but whose empirical feasibility often develops only during the course of centuries. To believe that a revolution is possible before its time is as naive as not noticing—when such a revolutionary process has begun—its empirical possibility. History matures with an objective rhythm that does not necessarily enter into personal biographies no matter how voluntaristically we might wish.

[17.3] POLITICAL POSTULATES AS CRITERIA FOR ORIENTING TRANSFORMATION

[17.3.1] The subject of "political postulates" is of the utmost importance at present, since many confuse logical possibility (that which could be thought without contradiction) with empirical possibility (that which could effectively be accomplished). Moreover, we must necessarily add to this the notion of "regulative ideas," which operate as criteria to orient action. Chinese navigators took their bearings at night by gazing at the North Star. This was a criterion for orientation, but no navigator sought to arrive empirically at the star, because to do so was empirically impossible. In politics there are "political postulates"—developed by Kant in his work after the *Critique of Judgment*—which can help to enlighten us regarding questions that are badly posed by a somewhat anarchist extreme Left.

[17.3.2] To repeat, a "political postulate" is a logically thinkable (possible) statement that remains *empirically* impossible but nevertheless serves to *orient* action. In every institutional sphere we will demonstrate the existence and usefulness of proposing certain postulates, but we cannot confuse these with the goals of action because they remain *empirically impossible*. Recall the proposed ideal of a "society without classes." This is a postulate: such a society is impossible, but by attempting to overcome the present class relation we discover the possibility for a form of social progress that, at the very least, rejects the domination of the present system (under the form of the bourgeois and working classes) and gives a critical meaning to class domination in the historical present. Formulating the postulate helps us to attempt to dissolve the existing classes, to thereby "approach" the classless society (which like the crossing of asymptotic lines is impossible by definition).

[17.3.3] Normative principles subjectively obligate political actors to fulfill the demands of the constitutive moments of political power, of liberation praxis, and of institutional transformation for the good of the *people*. On the other hand, postulates, which are not normative principles, help to *orient* praxis toward its goals and to transform institutions, thus fixing a horizon of empirically impossible realization but one that *opens up* a space of practical possibility beyond the current system (which tends to be interpreted as *natural* rather than *historical*). Postulates, then, function strategically to open up *new* possibilities.

[17.3.4] On the other hand, postulates need to be distinguished from political paradigms.[103] The liberal paradigm is not that of the welfare State, and the neoliberal paradigm, in turn, must be presently replaced by a new alternative paradigm. This alternative paradigm, in turn, must be distinguished from both the medium term (the next twenty-five years) and the long term: a *new political system* in a *new*, ecologically sustainable, transcapitalist and transmodern *civilization*, but in this we are speaking of more than fifty years and perhaps a century. Postulates allow for the opening of short-term paradigms into the long term.

TRANSFORMATION OF INSTITUTIONS IN THE MATERIAL SPHERE: "PERPETUAL LIFE" AND SOLIDARITY

[18.0.1] The *material* level ("material" as *content*) is that which refers always in the last instance to life. In *Origin of the Family* Engels writes the following splendid passage: "According to the materialistic interpretation[104] of history the last instance is the production and reproduction of immediate life [*unmittelbaren Lebens*] . . . the production of the means of existence, of food, clothing, and shelter."[105]

[18.0.2] Institutions created to reproduce life [» 7.3] always suffer an inevitable moment of crisis, of entropic erosion, of reversal in meaning. From having been created to advance life they begin to be parasitic upon that very life and to produce death. They have become fetishized. Thus it is time to transform them, replace them, and create new institutions that respond to the new historical moment of global human life.

[18.1] ECOLOGICAL TRANSFORMATIONS: "PERPETUAL LIFE"

[18.1.1] The *political postulate* on the ecological level—the field of relations between the living human being and its physical-natural terrestrial environment—could be expressed as follows: We must behave such that our actions and institutions allow for the existence of human life on planet Earth forever, perpetually![106] "Perpetual life" is the fundamental ecological-political postulate. Given that this is empirically impossible—since, while it might be a matter of millions of years, Earth will at some point cease to support life as a result of the cooling of the solar system—we are dealing with a criterion for political orientation that allows the following: that in all relations with the *terra mater* (the *pacha mama* of Quechua Incas) renewable resources be used before nonrenewable ones (like petroleum, gas, and all metals); that productive processes be developed that result in a minimum of *negative* ecological effects; that processes that allow for the *recycling* of components in the short term be privileged over those in the long term; and that expenses invested toward canceling out these negative effects of the productive process be accounted for as production costs of the commodities placed on the market.[107] As we might imagine, this would represent a greater revolution than any ever imagined by the civilizations that have existed up to the present.

[18.1.2] What I have said above could be reformulated even *more strictly* as follows: the use-rate of renewable resources should not surpass their rate of regeneration; the use-rate of nonrenewable resources should not surpass the rate at which renewable substitutes are invented; finally, the pollution rate should not be greater than the rate at which pollutants and waste are recycled, and this includes the reversal of the process of global warming and its causes—that is, the recuperation of past negative effects. In this sense, one could say that in its resources and negative effects, economics becomes a subsphere of ecology.

[18.1.3] Humanity has lived politically in an age of a total lack of awareness regarding the risk to life posed by the intervention of civilization on Earth. Fire, the mediation of all technical mediations, has transformed the atmosphere for the past 600,000 years through the emission of carbon dioxide, but agriculture has in the past ten years nearly finished off the oxygen-producing forests. As a result, when Donella Meadows et al. published *The Limits of Growth* in 1972, humanity began to gain consciousness of the political centrality of the possibility of the extinction of life on our planet. In the "Standard World Model Run," figure 35 of *The Limits of Growth*, the authors predicted that after the middle of the twenty-first century there would be population disaster as pollution reaches a peak and the process of industrial production declines. Later discoveries have shown that the issue is even more grave and the pace even more accelerated. Today we confront the reality of an absolute political irresponsibility (especially in the most polluting industrial country in the world, the United States) in the face of irreversible ecological effects (at least during the next few thousand years).

[18.1.4] Changing our attitude toward nature—which would entail a concomitant transformation on the level of modern institutions—brings us face-to-face with something much more radical than merely a different socio-historic project. In effect, the advent of Modernity has meant for five hundred years (since the *invasion* of America in 1492) not only the beginning of capitalism, colonialism, and Eurocentrism, but also the beginning of a type of civilization. Both the *ego conquiro* of Cortés and the *ego cogito* of Descartes's incorporeal soul devalued nature as a mere mechanical, geometrical *res extensa*. Quantity destroyed quality. What is necessary is an *Ecological Revolution* of a type never before dreamed of by any thinker of the nineteeth century or the twentieth. Is it not the case that capitalism, and even real existing socialism, have corresponded to a contempt for the *absolute dignity of life in general*, life as the prolongation and condition of our living bodies (as Marx puts it in the "Economic and Philosophical Manuscripts of 1844"[108])? Was it not the criteria of an "increase in the rate of profit" (in capitalism) and an "increase in the rate of production" (in real socialism) that brought us to this ecological cataclysm?

[18.1.5] The point is to imagine a *new, transmodern civilization* based on an absolute respect for life in general, and that of the human in particular, in which all other dimensions of existence must be reprogrammed on the basis of the postulate of "perpetual life." This task falls to *all political institutions* and demands their radical transformation.

[18.2] ECONOMIC TRANSFORMATIONS: THE "REALM OF FREEDOM"

[18.2.1] Marx formulated the economic postulate as the "Realm of Freedom." It could be expressed as follows: We must operate in the economic field in such a manner as to always transform the productive processes toward the horizon of *zero work* (W^0). A *perfect* economy would not be one of *perfect competition* (as Hayek believes) but rather one in which technology has replaced all human labor (*zero work*: logically possible, empirically impossible). In this scenario, humanity has been liberated from the harsh discipline of work and is able to enjoy cultural goods (the subsequent material field, discussed in the following section). In a text full of anti-economistic humanism, we find the following:

> The realm of freedom [*Reich der Freiheit*] actually begins only where labour, which is determined by necessity and mundane consideration ceases, . . . it lies *beyond the sphere of actual material production.*[109] Just as the savage must wrestle with Nature to satisfy his wants, to *maintain and reproduce life*, so must civilized man . . . under *all possible modes of production.*[110] . . . Freedom in this field can only consist in socialized man, the associated producers, rationally regulating[111] their interchange with Nature, bringing it under their *common control [gemeinschaftliche]*,[112] instead of being ruled by it as by the blind [power of capital];[113] and achieving this with the *least expenditure of energy*[114] and under conditions *most favorable to, and worthy of, their human nature.*[115] But it nonetheless still remains a realm of necessity.[116] *Beyond* it begins that development of human [cultural] energy which is an end in itself, the true realm of freedom. . . . The shortening of the working-day is its basic prerequisite.[117]

[18.2.2] The objective of the economy is human life, and this goal should be achieved with the least possible use of that life ("shortening of the working-day"), and not to the contrary through an increase in the work of some (who suffer), unemployment for others (who die in poverty), and the imposition of the increasing accumulation of profit as an objective of the economy, which sacrifices with it all of humanity (as victim of misery) and life on Earth (due to the ecological issues discussed above).[118] The *absolute limit* of capital and of the Modern Age of humanity—and as a result the need to transition to a new human age—consists in the extinction of the human species as a form of collective suicide, in the ways indicated above (misery and ecological destruction).

[18.2.3] In other words, the transformation of economic systems and institutions (within the economic field) falls under the responsibility of politics insofar as these intersect with the political field (and its concrete institutional systems) and distort all moments of politics (as the citizen living in misery lacks the political conditions for autonomy, freedom, and responsibility demanded by their rights, and as the extinction of life is very evidently the end of politics). *Intervention* in the systems of the economic field is part of the political function—against capitalist and liberal "economism of the market"[119]—once we clearly understand the impossibility of the market producing equilibrium and justice for all, and avoiding the accumulation of wealth in the hands of the few and an increase in poverty among the great majority. The possibility of a nonwork income for all families within a State as a right of citizenship should be studied and implemented.[120]

[18.2.4] The normative principle governing *interventions* into the operations and institutions of the (currently capitalist) economic system should always be that the production, reproduction, and enhancement of human life serves as the criterion for evaluating the productive process and its effects as a totality, including the market, national and transnational capital, financial capital, etc.: "[It is] a political right to *intervene in the market* and, as such, to *intervene* in the power of private, transnational bureaucracies. The point is not to revive centralized or totalized planning, but certainly global planning and management of the economy as a whole."[121]

[18.2.5] At the same time, social movements—the *people*—have started from critical situations of extreme poverty produced by an orthodox, neoliberal "economic fundamentalism" (as even Soros calls it) and then have moved on to invent a growing "solidarity economy."[122] This is a dimension to be borne in mind, because it was from the interstices of medieval feudalism in Europe that the cities were born as despised, secondary places where serfs worked with their own hands and created a *new* civilization. Do we not find ourselves in a similar situation?

[18.2.6] Concrete transformations of the various moments of the institutional economic system, which fall within the responsibility of politics, must be the object of detailed developments from the perspective of a political and economic model of coresponsibility with movements and political parties, their concrete projects, and their strategic proposals. What we have said here only serves to *situate* the question in its proper context.

[18.2.7] A fundamental criterion that is imposed by necessity on Latin America is the defense of natural resources against the advancing domination of extractive, productive, and financial transnationals, which will leave entire populations without the future resources to reproduce their own lives. Future generations will hold us responsible for our failure to defend these resources!

The struggle for water in Bolivia represents a fundamental battle over life itself, over *bare life*, over the safeguarding of the rights of a *people* to survival. In its triumph, life too has triumphed.

[18.3] CULTURAL TRANSFORMATIONS: THE TRANS-MODERN PLURIVERSE

[18.3.1] The (economic) "Realm of Freedom" opens up the material sphere of culture within politics, since "free time" is time that should be available for cultural creation and not merely for the passive absorption of advertising propaganda from the mediaocracy. Liberal politics tacitly and Eurocentrically supposes that Western culture represents a perfect, universal civilization, which in its modern development should be imposed upon all other "savage," underdeveloped, or backward cultures. Modernity began with the conquest of the Caribbean and of Mexico, a process that produced a terrible cultural genocide that destroyed the great millennial cultures of the Aztecs, Mayas, and Incas, and later those of the Bantus, Chinese, Hindustanis, Muslims, etc. Capitalism, too, presupposes Western culture as the only universal: its commodities are Western cultural products that carry within them the values of that culture, imperceptible and invisible in their phenomenal form as an automobile, a Hollywood film, a hamburger, a mode of dress, or a brand of shoes. Standard commodities have been understood through European and North American criteria, leading to industrialization and the destruction of old, precapitalist artisan production in European and other cultures.

[18.3.2] Politics must equally *intervene*—and has always done so, at least since the bourgeois revolutions in France or England—on the cultural level, because Modernity has made us accustomed to scorning the culture of the periphery and venerating all that is "modern" and Western. There must have been a German artist who discovered the beauty and the artistic merit of the ruins and other conserved objects from the high Mayan civilization. Scorning what is one's own—Malinchism[123]—is the suicidal attitude of a colonized, Creole elite.

[18.3.3] The recuperation and affirmation of one's own dignity, culture, language, religion,[124] ethical values, and respectful relation to nature stands in opposition to the liberal political ideal of a homogeneous egalitarianism among citizens. When equality destroys diversity, it becomes necessary to defend cultural *difference*. When the use of cultural difference serves to dominate others, it becomes necessary to defend the *Equality* of human dignity. The *peoples*, nations, and ethnic and social groups that inhabit a single territory under the institutional organization of a Political Society (a State) have been traditionally defined as members of a monocultural political totality. In reality, however, no modern State (Spain, the United Kingdom, France, Italy, etc.) contains only a single nation, ethnic group, or language but rather embraces various cultures with their varying languages, histories, and even religions. The cultural unity of the modern State is a fiction. In reality, these are multicultural States. The point, then, is to recognize the multicultural character of the political community and begin an education in intercultural dialogue that is respectful of differences. In Latin America, States like Mexico, Peru, Bolivia, and Guatemala, which shelter in their hearts great millennial cultures and pillars of human history, must change their constitutions, their legal systems, their judicial practice, their systems of education and health care, and their exercise of delegated political power on the municipal level, granting autonomy to indigenous communities on all cultural and political levels.

[18.3.4] During the Zapatista uprising in Chiapas, President Zedillo spoke of the rebellion as an attack on sovereignty. First, sovereignty belongs to the political community, the *people*, not to the State. Second, indigenous communities are and have always possessed—since prior to the *invasion* by Cortés— inalienable popular sovereignty. To rise up in defense of indigenous culture is a right that predates the Mexican State itself. We need a Cultural Revolution— as Evo Morales proclaims in Bolivia—in which each community is able to affirm its culture, speak its language, exercise its rights, defend its security, elect its own authorities according to its own customs (at least on the municipal level), arrange its own system of education and health care, its own economic system, etc.

[18.3.5] Moreover, the *people* need to be educated in a pedagogical system that overcomes Eurocentrism in all branches of knowledge (and first of all in history)—a system that coherently explains the long and complex plurinational history of Latin America within world history. There must be education in pluricultural ethical-normative principles, a technical and economic education appropriate to the level of development, which should be autonomous and primarily inward focused in order to then be able to compete with some chance of success.

[18.3.6] This education must stand in solidarity with those most in need, the victims of the present ecological, economic, and cultural systems, the poorest, and this solidarity must surpass the mere fraternity of the bourgeois revolution; instead, it must be a solidarity with the victims of institutions that must be transformed. When the political actor assumes as "friends" the excluded, the "enemies" of the system become friends and former friends become new enemies. Like a hostage to the system—as Levinas would say—the political actor who is responsible to the Other is persecuted. Those who occupy the position of the poor, in their defense, become an object for punishment by the powerful. The political actor who assumes politics as a vocation—knowing that this noble pursuit places the poor, the last, at the forefront of its service—confronts persecution as glory.

[18.3.7] Hermann Cohen—the founder of the Marburg school of philosophy in which Heidegger studied—has a beautiful expression of the fertility of solidarity, which extends even to the theoretical level: "The method[125] consists of knowing how to situate oneself in the position of the poor and, from there, to carry out a diagnosis of the pathology of the State."[126]

TRANSFORMATION OF INSTITUTIONS IN THE SPHERE
OF DEMOCRATIC LEGITIMACY: IRRUPTION OF NEW RIGHTS:
"PERPETUAL PEACE" AND ALTERITY

19

[19.1] THE POSTULATE OF "PERPETUAL PEACE":
RESPONSIBILITY FOR THE EXCLUDED: ALTERITY

[19.1.1] Beyond the *Equality* of the bourgeois revolution we find a responsibility toward *Alterity*—toward the rights distinct to the Other. Beyond the political community of equals (white, property-owning, metropolitan, abstract, elite citizens) we find the exploited, the excluded, the nonequals (citizens who are nonwhite, poor, postcolonial, and differentiated by culture, sex, age), and the popular masses. New rights take these *people* into account.

[19.1.2] The operative postulate in the sphere of legitimacy is that of "perpetual peace," which is logically thinkable but empirically impossible to carry out. As an orienting criterion, however, this idea opens up to us the horizon of being able to resolve all conflicts in a nonviolent manner (as could have been the case with the unjust and useless wars carried out by the United States in Afghanistan and Iraq, which resulted from the temptation of a militarized power lacking normative principles). "Perpetual peace" defines discursive reason as being in charge of arriving at agreements: fairness in the face of violence, fulfilling material demands [» 18], and participation under equal conditions. To banish violence as a means for reaching agreements is the proper goal of democratic legitimacy.

[19.1.3] Material interests (social, economic, ecological, cultural, etc.) determine the actor who participates in the institutions of legitimacy (elections, representation, constitutional assemblies, legal systems, congresses, judges, etc.

[» 8.1–2]). By definition, however, no system of legitimacy or democracy can be *perfect*. Inevitably, then, this leaves many citizens excluded, because they often fall outside the definition of the citizen as such, as was the case for wage laborers in the theory of Locke, for women prior to the suffragettes, and for mestizos, indigenous, and slaves considered unequal by emancipated Latin American Creoles, etc. As a result, the *Equality* of the bourgeois political community has historically *excluded* the majority of the population.

[19.1.4] By solidarity in the legal sphere, I mean a responsibility for those who do not have rights (or have not been granted them). The affirmation of the *Alterity* of the other is not the same as liberal Equality. Even the struggle for the recognition of the other *as equal* (aspiring toward its *incorporation* within the Same) is different from the struggle for the recognition of the Other *as other* (which thereby aspires toward a *new legal system* subsequent to the recognition of Difference). The affirmation of Alterity is much more radical than the homogeneity of the *modern* citizen, as we are speaking of the institutionalization of a heterogeneous, differentiated legality that respects diverse juridical practices. For example, in modern law—with its long history that begins with Roman or medieval law—those who kill another are imprisoned, sometimes for life. Among Mayans in Chiapas, those who kill another member of the community are punished, in the first place, by having to cultivate the land of the deceased in order to feed the family that has been left without sustenance. The Mayans demonstrate the irrationality of modern legality, since in the latter the murderer and the deceased leave *two families* without food, thereby punishing the unprotected families rather than the one who carried out the act. On the other hand, the victim gains nothing from the imprisonment of his or her murderer, but rather loses a great deal through the poverty and misery of his or her family. In this way we can see the superiority of one penal system over another.

[19.2] TRANSFORMATION OF THE SYSTEM OF RIGHT: NEW RIGHTS AND JUDICIAL POWER

[19.2.1] Systems of right are historical (2 in figure 12), and they have suffered continuous change. The question is one of defining the criteria of those changes in order to determine which among these rights are *perennial*, which

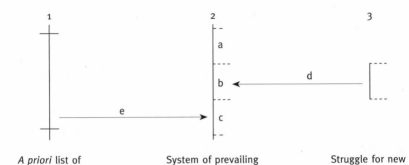

A *priori* list of
natural rights

System of prevailing
rights and laws

Struggle for new
a posteriori rights

Figure 12. NATURAL LAW, PREVAILING LAW, AND THE STRUGGLE FOR NEW RIGHTS

are *new*, and which are *discarded* as belonging to a past epoch. All three types have always existed within all collections or legal codes since the Mesopotamian collections of laws at the end of the third millennium B.C. However, even today we still speak of the logic of incorporating new rights, those that irrupt as conflicts or demands based on the unsatisfied needs of *new* social movements—the struggles by the *people* for the recognition of *new* rights.

[19.2.2] The traditional solution, to have an external reference point from which to call into question *positive* law (the prevailing body of law: 2 in figure 12), consists in affirming the existence of a "natural law" (*1* in figure 12), which would be like a list of rights proper to the human being as such, universally speaking. This Eurocentric solution (as it refers back to the Hellenic and Roman worlds by way of the Germanic-Latin world of modern Europe) is theoretically unsustainable, since what happens *historically* is that new rights are discovered (*3* in figure 12). In the traditional understanding, such a new right would need to be discovered in the a priori list of natural laws but, in reality, the absence of right within the list of natural laws, *prior* to its historical discovery, demonstrates that natural laws are only recognized post factum (*after the "fact"*) and through a struggle by those who discover such rights empirically.

[19.2.3] As a result, *natural law* is an unnecessary and useless metaphysical hypothesis. In reality, the prevailing right always exists as given and as *positive*

(2 in figure 12), and *new* rights (*3* in figure 12) are not "taken" from a list of natural law but, to the contrary, emerge from popular struggles (*arrow d*). *New* social movements gain consciousness—on the basis of their living and suffering corporeality—of being excluded victims of the legal system in that aspect that substantively defines their liberation or critical praxis. British feminist suffragettes discover that women *do not vote* to elect political representatives. This negativity is lived as "*lacking-the-right-to,*" a right *lived* as necessary but one that is *positively* nonexistent for the intersubjectivity of these conscious women, who have arrived at the conclusion of what Freire would call a "process of critical consciousness formation."

[19.2.4] That is, these *new rights* are imposed a posteriori by the struggling movements who discover the "lack-of" as a "new-right-to" certain practices that were ignored or prohibited by the existing right. At the outset, this new right exists only in the subjectivity of the oppressed and excluded, but after the triumph of the rebellious movement this new right is imposed *historically* and is added to the list of positive rights (*b* in moment 2 in figure 12).

[19.2.5] At the same time that new rights are being incorporated into the existing system of rights, other rights—pertaining to a prior era in the history of the political community, the *people*—fall into disrepute (*c* in moment 2 of figure 12). The "coercive right" (*ius dominativus*) of the feudal lord over the serf (*arrow e*) disappears in capitalist Modernity, and the same can be said of the rights of the slaveholder vis-à-vis the slave.

[19.2.6] There is final institution, as old as those that enact laws (whether it be the king, the senate, etc.), that closes the circle of the system of right as a "government-by-law": the judiciary. Occasionally, it is the king or the senate itself that fulfill the exercise of judging the accused in accordance with the law. Already in the *Codex* of Mesopotamia in the third millennium B.C. the function of judges was clearly stipulated. In Modernity, the judicial function—as a *Judicial Power* that plays a proper role with respect to *Legislative* and *Executive Power*—comes to be independent of the other two, thereby permitting mutual control. Judicial autonomy is essential for the "government-by-law," as it judges conduct and institutions in light of the legal system and promulgated laws and prevents "taking justice into one's own hands," thereby overcoming the barbarous law of "an eye for an eye, a tooth for a tooth" that predates law but is still used in our time by terrorist States. The corruption entailed by the latter is fatal because it compromises the entire political order.

[19.27] Impunity weakens the power of the *people*, because it is in the name of the latter that law must be enforced and injustice punished. As a result, it is necessary to continue to develop the autonomy of Judicial Power, making it the object of direct popular elections by legitimate bodies of attorneys and the intervention of *Citizen Power* (not an election by those who need to be judged—i.e., the Legislative and Executive Powers).

[19.3] REPRESENTATIVE DEMOCRACY LINKED WITH PARTICIPATORY DEMOCRACY

[19.3.1] If there were always direct democracy, as in the classic moment of the Venetian Republic and its Great Council (a modified form of the modern English State of the seventeenth century), legitimacy would be justified de facto, because everyone would have participated in discussing the consensus (once they had voted to accept the majority as a necessary institution, because even in direct democracy unanimity cannot always be presupposed). But once we accept that there exist hundreds of thousands or millions of citizens in a political community or a *people*, then *representation* becomes an inevitable and necessary institution.

[19.3.2] The political postulate is enunciated in this case as the aspiration to an *identity* of the representative and the represented [representative equals represented]. This identity—as perfect transparency in an intersubjective relation between the many represented and the representative, the politician by vocation, profession, or occasion—is logically thinkable but empirically *impossible*. Given the *need* for representation and the *impossibility* of its *absolute* transparency, it is necessary to accept the finitude of the human condition that manifests in *all* political institutions (which as a result are not intrinsically corrupt but can become corrupted easily),[127] and as a result to also accept the struggle to always reinvent, improve, and transform forms of representation such that these become ever closer to the represented. In experimenting empirically with popular demands, understanding them profoundly, and formulating ways to satisfy them; in fidelity to the truth of this project of service;

and in continuously informing the represented, the representative fulfills the regulative criterion to always achieve a better form of representation.

[19.3.3] For this, the Constitution must create *participatory* institutions [» 20] (from the bottom up) that serve to control institutions of *representation* (from the top down), thus privileging such instruments as neighborhood communities and political parties. When the party becomes corrupted—when it wields for its own advantage the power delegated to it, as though that power belonged to the bureaucracy—the political system as a totality becomes corrupted. This explains the present disrepute of political parties in Latin America and elsewhere. These, however, remain necessary, as a "school" of political opinion, ideology, and material and administrative projects to be rationally and empirically justified. Without parties, the best possible leaders of the *people* would have neither enlightened nor critical opinions. They would succumb to spontaneism when confronted by bureaucracies, which was the inevitable situation of those real socialisms that neglected the need for multiple parties.

[19.3.4] It is therefore necessary to create a fourth Power, which has not yet existed within the State. In chapter 4 of title 2 of the 1999 *Constitution of the Bolivarian Republic of Venezuela*—"On Political Rights and the Popular Referendum"—article 62 states the following: "All citizens have the right to *participate* freely in public affairs, directly or through their elected representatives. *Popular participation* in the formation, execution, and *control* of public management is the necessary means to achieve a protagonism which guarantees full development, individually and collectively." To which article 70 adds: "The following are means for the *participation* and protagonism of the *people* in exercising its sovereignty in the political realm: elections to public posts, *referenda, popular consultations, revoking mandates, and legislative, constitutional, and constituent initiative, open councils, and citizen assemblies* whose decisions will be binding."

[19.3.5] In effect, title 4 of chapter 4 deals with "Public Power." In the second part of article 136, we read what constitutes a world-historical novelty in human political practice up to the present: "National Public Power is divided into *Legislative, Executive, Judicial, Citizen, and Electoral Powers.*"

[19.3.6] Title 4 of chapter 4 deals with "Citizen Power." This Power is exercised though the "Republican Moral Consensus" (article 273), composed of the Ombudsman, the Public Minister, and the General Comptroller of the

Republic. Its members are elected by a Petition Evaluation Committee that names the Republican Moral Consensus, which then presents a group of three (one chosen by each member) to the General Assembly, which in turn selects one of these candidates by a two-thirds vote. If not elected by the General Assembly, the election "is subjected to a popular consultation" (article 279). What is most interesting is that there exists the possibility for a "popular consultation," and this is an important precedent for participation. Regardless, the Executive and Legislative Powers do not initiate the procedure of this election of members to the fourth Power, but this election is still not direct and popular. It is still a halfway step.

[19.3.7] Referenda, popular consultations, revocable mandates, Citizen and Electoral Power [» 20], the manner of electing the judges to the Supreme Court from *Citizen Power* and Civil Society organizations, the fact that a simple citizen can initiate the process of passing a law—these all give us an idea of a new political spirit. This spirit is one of *citizen participation* in a democracy in which the *people* have sovereignty that they can exercise permanently and not only in those volcanic eruptions that are the elections every six years. *Representative* democracy (which tends to be a movement *from the top down*) needs to be linked with *participatory* democracy (as a movement exerting control *from the bottom up*).

[19.3.8] For Arendt, here agreeing with Marx's celebration of the 1870 Paris Commune, the direct democracy of groups organized on the county level[128] in the United States (a necessary institution for Jefferson)—and represented in the Bolivarian Constitution by open councils, neighborhood groupings, base communities, etc.—operates as an institution for face-to-face participation by citizens, which if lacking, for Jefferson, would lead to the corruption of those institutions foreseen in the Constitution of the United States.[129] That is, it would be necessary to create new participatory institutions in order to control representation.

[19.3.9] It might seem strange that *participation*—of the simple citizen, of social organizations, and of Civil Society—needs equally to be organized through institutions. Critical-political realism is not afraid to create these institutions, but in this case they should not respond to the interests of Political Parties (nor to the "political class"), since they need to serve those

| Representative | a | ⟶ | Participatory |
| institutions | ⟵ | b | institutions |

Figure 13. THE MUTUAL INSTITUTIONAL DETERMINATION OF REPRESENTATION AND PARTICIPATION

configurations that control the representative institutions that are structured principally not only around Legislative and Executive Power but also the Judicial (whose mandate *Citizen Power*, in very serious cases, could also revoke). It will become necessary to create a new and more complex State structure, with mutual determinations[130] (see figure 13) by *representation* and *participation* within governability, in order to avoid the *monopoly* of political parties and the political class in the management of the delegated exercise of power, against which, on December 20, 2001, the *people* shouted: "Out with them all!" This clamor is a reminder that power belongs to the *people*, which appears in certain limit moments *as a people* in a "State of Rebellion."

[19.4] THE "RIGHT TO TRUTHFUL INFORMATION" AND THE DEMOCRATIC-POPULAR REGULATION OF THE MEDIAOCRACY

[19.4.1] Public opinion interprets political events: it is the final Judge of politics, politicians, leaders, candidates, public affairs, etc., playing the role fulfilled by Osiris in the grand chamber of the Egyptian goddess of justice, Ma'at, a narrative originating in Memphis more than five thousand years ago. Here we are speaking of nothing less than a hermeneutic "evaluative judgment" of the representative, and those who form and shape this judgment bear in its totality the *last instance* of political responsibility. This judgment is put approximately as follows: "He/she was a bad leader!" or "He/she is an excellent candidate!" Thanks to such *judgments*, the former passes negatively into history and the latter is elected. The communication media—large transnational corporations linked to foreign capital in peripheral and postcolonial countries, with their interests often opposing those of the oppressed *peoples—form these value judgments*. They have an immense *power* that stands behind all of the Powers of the State: that is, *a Superpower*. A media magnate was until recently prime minister of Italy: this is the domination of the media economy *over* politics.

[19.4.2] The task is to *democratize* communication media. Every university, association, municipality, union, ethnic group, neighborhood, etc. could have its own television or radio program, or written press. The rupturing of this monopoly in the hands of the few will return "public opinion" to its central role in the system of legitimation, because the decisions, elections, projects, etc. are determined in the last instance behind the veil of subjectivity, when one "has made his or her *own* judgment" about what to decide and what to do. Consensus presupposes individual *prudence* (*phronesis*, as the ancients put it), and the mediaocracy impacts each singular consciousness in the privacy of his or her own home and everyday life, thus shaping her or him much more profoundly than any educational institution.

[19.4.3] But not only do we need to allow the symmetrical participation of popular media, we also need to define a hitherto nonpromulgated right: namely, *the right* of the citizen to *truthful information*. For this right to have a real and compelling effect would require the institutionalization of a tribunal—not merely for "freedom of the press" (which legitimately defends the media *from* the State)[131]—but equally of the truthfulness of this information, thereby defending the citizen *against* misleading, false, deceptive, or tendentious information. The right to respond is one aspect of this right, but there are others in need of development. Such rights should be accorded a chapter of future constitutions, since dependent countries suffer a constant attack from the distortion of messages by the *mediaocracy of transnational media corporations*, based in the metropolitan States at the core of the world system (as Wallerstein or Chomsky would put it).

20

TRANSFORMATION OF INSTITUTIONS IN THE SPHERE OF FEASIBILITY: THE "DISSOLUTION OF THE STATE"? LIBERATION

[20.1] THE POSTULATE OF THE "DISSOLUTION OF THE STATE"

[20.1.1] The question of whether or not it is possible to "change the world without taking power" has from the outset been posed incorrectly. *Power* is not "taken" as though it were a thing, an object at hand, or a well-bound package. Power is a faculty belonging to the political community [» 2], to the *people* [» 12]. The power that *appears* to be "taken" is merely the mediations or institutions of the delegated exercise [» 3] of this fundamental power. If the delegated exercise of power takes the form of *obedience* [» 4], this power qua service is just, adequate, and necessary. If one were to "take" control of already corrupted institutions, or structures of *fetishized* power [» 5], this exercise would not operate to the benefit of the community, the *people*. As a result, one cannot "change the world" through such a corrupted exercise, as should be obvious by now. The subject, then, has been posed in a confusing manner. To simplify, we could say that it is the position of Bakunin, of anarchism, that all institutions are repressive [» 7].

[20.1.2] When an honest representative of the political community, the *people*, is delegated for the exercise of institutional power, they must in the first place not merely fulfill the already institutionally defined and structured functions of power (*potestas*) [» 3]. It remains always necessary to consider whether or not these given institutions truly *serve* to satisfy the demands of the community, the *people*, and social movements. If they do not serve these demands, they need to be transformed. Chávez changed the Constitution at the outset of his delegated exercise of power, as did Evo Morales. That is, the *package* of State institutions (*potestas*) needs to be untied and changed as a whole by conserving what is sustainable and eliminating what is unjust—thereby creating the new. Power (as *potestas*) is not "taken" en bloc. It is reconstituted and exercised critically in view of the material satisfaction of needs, in fulfillment of the normative demands of democratic legitimacy, and within empirical political possibility. But, to be clear, without the *obediential* exercise of delegated institutional power *the world cannot feasibly be changed.* To attempt to do so is little more than abstract and apolitical moralism and idealism, which clearly results from practical and theoretical confusions. However, these quasi-anarchists do indeed remind us that institutions become fetishized and always need to be transformed, as Marx points out.

[20.1.3] On the level of *strategic feasibility*, in order to change the world one needs to rely on an extraordinarily healthy political postulate: that of the "dissolution of the State." This postulate can be put approximately as follows: We must operate in such a way as to tend toward the (empirically impossible) identity of representation with the represented, in such a way that State institutions become always increasingly transparent, effective, simplified, etc. Such a condition would not, however, be a "minimal State"—in either the right-wing version of Nozick or the left-wing version of Bakunin—but rather a "subjectified State," in which the institutions become diminished due to the increasingly shared responsibility by *all citizens* ("We are all the State!").[132] This would need to proceed alongside the application of the *electronic* revolution in order to reduce almost to zero the time and space required for citizen participation,[133] in terms of collecting the opinion of the citizenry to constitute a consensus or carry out bureaucratic procedures. This would be a *virtual State* with decentralized offices, managed by Web sites, and the State of the future would be so different from that of the present that many of its most bureaucratic, opaque, and bloated institutions would have disappeared . . . *It would appear* that the State no longer exists, but it will be more present than ever as the normative responsibility of each citizen toward the others. This is the criterion of orientation that follows from the postulate of the "dissolution of the State."

[20.2] TRANSFORMATION OF THE STATE: CITIZEN POWER, ELECTORAL POWER, AND CIVIL SOCIETY

[20.2.1] At the root of the transformation of the State we confront the problem of constructing a *participatory democracy* in which the *people* exercise *control* over delegated, administrative, legislative, executive, and judicial power, such that these satisfy the demands of the citizens, the social movements, and the *people* itself. The difficulty of exerting this control rests on the creation of special institutions to effectively exercise the indicated control and in the means granted to fulfill these ends. But, as a result, these institutions must enjoy the autonomy and authority granted by citizen participation.

[20.2.2] In the context of the formal transitional democracies—organized in Latin America simultaneous to the removal since 1983 of the totalitarian governments imposed by the U.S. Department of State—the political class has exercised an increasing monopoly over the delegated exercise of State power (*potestas*, or Gramsci's restricted State) through political parties. It is necessary to open up the political game, allowing for the *permanent* praxis of Civil Society and social movements through the creation of parallel institutions from the bottom up—for example, groups below the municipal level (such as neighborhood groups and public assemblies) built on direct democratic participation. Their delegates would then organize on the municipal, state, or provincial level, and elect from among themselves the members of *Citizen Power*, which itself can elect other levels of delegation.

[20.2.3] *Citizen Power*, which already exists in the Bolivarian Constitution [» 19.34]—but which still lacks powerful organization *from below*—would be like a controlling power (a *political* solicitor with maximal capacities) that could even convoke a consultation of all of the citizens in order to revoke the mandate of a member of the other four Powers (including *Electoral Power*). Or it could convoke a popular referendum regarding some urgent question (stipulating strictly the conditions of possibility for such proceedings). There needs to exist much more than merely a "Republican Moral Council" [» 19.36].

[20.2.4] It is evident that the greater the complexity of the State structures, the more difficult *governability* becomes, especially in periods of crisis. For this reason, there needs to be a clear institutional intelligence in order to exert control and to interrogate leaders without falling into chaos and anomie. In any case, if information is provided electronically regarding all actions of representatives (salaries, expenses, meetings, daily orders, publications, projects, consultations, etc.), and if these representatives are in frequent contact with the represented, then *Citizen Power* will remind them of the demand for transparency and responsibility of representatives for the rights and the satisfaction of the demands of the represented.

[20.2.5] For their part, civil society associations and those of the properly social sphere thereby acquire significant importance, and as such they should be equally regulated in their constitution, in the democratic procedures of their assemblies, in the legitimate elections of their authorities, etc. Organized Civil Society should participate in the formation of *Citizen Power* and *Electoral Power* and, through their specific professional associations, in the elections of *Judicial Power*. They might also compose part of a jury in all trials, as occurs in distinct forms in the United States and Norway (and in the latter, alongside all judges there is always a simple citizen who observes the judge in the name of Civil Society).

[20.2.6] To all this we must add that, since autonomy should be granted to indigenous communities on at least the municipal level, such communities should also autonomously, collectively, and through shared sovereignty, as said above, organize their educational and health systems, public works, property system, police force, and even the enforcement of an ancestral juridical system (if they had one, with the possibility of fulfilling their own penal code and even the naming of judges according to their own customs). The provincial or national State should collect taxes and assign specific resources for the *self-management* of municipal communities that would operate with constitutional authority. The recognition of pluriculturalism—of free religious freedom in a postsecular world and of a diversity of *official* languages and economic, political, and educational systems—must be clearly affirmed.

[20.3] GOVERNABILITY AND LIBERATION:
THE CRITICAL-POLITICAL JUSTICE CLAIM

[20.3.1] This *new* politics is to be not only measured by a change in the property system but also by the "modes of appropriation" of economic and cultural surplus regulated through new participatory political institutions.[134] And this is a result of the increase in the citizen's free time for culture, a decrease in consumption (for ecological reasons of increasing the Earth's resources and decreasing the residual effects of production and consumption), and clearly a decrease in hours spent working on the way to the "Realm of Freedom." Progress is not measured quantitatively by GDP (with mercantile measurements in dollars) but rather by the subjective satisfaction of *capabilities* (to use Amartya Sen's term),[135] which requires a new civilizational paradigm politically governed by the demands of production, reproduction, and development of human life, that is, ecologically, economically, and culturally.

[20.3.2] Although it may be more complex, the "political system" that relies on broad participation enjoys a greater degree of legitimacy. When there exists a maximum social consensus, moreover, costs decline to a minimum, even in terms of the economic cost of services. The good leader is not afraid of participation but keeps an eye on governability. We often hear about the contradiction between democracy—especially participatory democracy—and governability. The "tough hand" of dictatorship appears superficially to represent the strong presence of a leader who imposes governability. But repression, domination, the lack of liberty and participation—these all weaken power (*potentia*), and as a result the leader loses footing, lacks support, and must enforce obedience against the will of popular demands. Hence, expenses for the army, the police, and the bureaucracy increase. On the other hand, the leader who knows how to awaken solidarity, responsibility, and the symmetrical participation of the oppressed and excluded—especially of all those already integrated into the political community—makes their conduct more governable. Governability and the symmetrical participation of the affected go hand in hand on all levels.

[20.3.3] In proportion to the fulfillment of the indicated material demands —alongside a growing and symmetrical participation (which increases legitimacy, but also makes the political system more complex) and intelligent technical feasibility (which opens up for us a new era of politics on all levels of State mediation, using satellite and electronic communication for the benefit of popular movements and citizens)—a political culture develops in which representatives can claim a certain *critical political justice claim*.

[20.3.4] I call this *"critical"* to draw a parallel with what in ethics we call the "critical goodness claim."[136] For the practical subject (ethical, political, economic, educational, sexual, etc.), to "claim" means to be able to publicly defend the reasons given for an action—reasons that must fulfill material conditions (of life), formal conditions (of validity or legitimacy), and feasibility (to be physically, technically, and economically *possible*, etc.). If these conditions are fulfilled, one could say that this is a "good act," but there exists a vast gulf between the "good" and the "goodness claim." To be "good" in the full sense is impossible for human finitude, and as a result the most that can be done is to say: "I believe that I have honestly fulfilled the (three indicated) ethical conditions and therefore I *make a claim to goodness.*" To "claim" is not "to be" (good). Those with an honest *claim* to goodness necessarily know that their act, as imperfect, will inevitably have *negative* effects. But since they have an "honest claim," they will have little difficulty accepting responsibility for this negative effect (as a practical mistake, again always possible given human finitude), and they will therefore be better prepared to *correct it* immediately (using the same principles that set the indicated conditions as the criteria for correction).

[20.3.5] So the citizen, the political representative, can have a *"critical political justice claim"*[137] with respect to his or her actions and the fulfillment of the delegated exercise of power. Those fulfilling the noble vocation of politics should be concerned with always maintaining this "honest claim," and while this does not mean that they do not make mistakes or have negative effects— since this is empirically impossible—it does imply that such mistakes should be unintentional. Moreover, this aspiration means that immediately upon discovering these (almost always thanks to one's enemies), the representative must undertake the normative task (which others would call ethical) of *correcting* that mistake.

[20.3.6] The "just" actor, the honest politician, who has a serious and continuous "*critical* political justice claim," who intends to work as he or she *ought to* do normatively as political habit, knows perfectly well how to recognize the *unintentional* negative effects of his or her actions. Such individuals might say: "In my place, who could avoid ever making a mistake?" That is, "*let he who is without sin cast the first stone.*" But if they immediately recognize and correct this concrete, unintentional mistake they have committed, they thereby *demonstrate* through this very correction that they are just and that they *maintain* an uninterrupted critical and political justice claim.

[20.3.7] In this *twentieth thesis* on feasibility, I would like to point out that this sphere of possible transformations (including revolutions) is situated within the strict space of *liberation* from an oppressive or exclusionary state of affairs. As such, these transformations are in accordance with a praxis of liberation. It is true that the bourgeois Revolution spoke of *liberty*, but what is necessary now is to subsume that liberty and speak instead of *liberation* (as in North American pragmatism, one does not speak of *truth* but rather of verification). So now we do not refer to liberty but instead to liber-*ation* as a process, as the negation of a point of departure, and as a tension pressing toward a point of arrival. We must therefore transform the postulate of the bourgeois Revolution expressed in the proclamation of "Equality, Fraternity, Liberty!" (through the rebellion of oppressed and excluded *peoples* of the periphery in their struggles for the Second Emancipation) into the new expression of "Alterity, Solidarity, Liberation!"

[20.3.8] All that has been said here has been necessarily framed within a spirit of Latin American unity—an integration that will permanently overcome the Organization of American States, a geopolitical organization representing North American domination. This unity has already begun with the signing of the Community of Latin American Pueblos on December 8, 2004, in Cuzco. The destiny of national States needs today to be integrated into confederated wholes like that achieved in the Constitutional Treaty of the European Union.[138] Europe is a political example in this respect for our cultural and political continent, the future of which is anticipated by the existence of Mercosur and the integration movements in South America, to which Mexico, Central America, and the Caribbean must join in the near future, thereby turning their backs on treaties with the Empire of the North, which thinks only of its own interests and cares little for those of the other participants.

1   This book is a synthesis of and an introduction to my three-volume work on *Política de la Liberación*.

2   I exclude Carlos Salinas de Gortari because he was not elected, but was instead a vulgar usurper.

1   Throughout this work, the bracketed arrow and number indicate the thesis in which the subject is discussed in more detail.

2   See Bourdieu, *Questions de sociologie*; *L'Ontologie politique de Martin Heidegger*; and *Les règles de l'art*.

3   See Luhmann, *Die Politik der Gesellschaft*.

4   The "world of everyday life" (*Lebenswelt*) is not the space colonized by systems but rather the whole within which component systems of that "everyday life" exist.

5   On nodes, see Castells, *The Information Age*. On the many definitions of "subjectivity," "intersubjectivity," and so forth, see my "Sobre el sujeto y la intersubjetividad," in *Hacia una filosofía colítica crítica*, 319.

6   The "impossible" is that which surpasses the horizon of a field and transforms it into an *alternative practice*.

7   Clausewitz, *On War*, book 2, chapter 2.

8   [*Standard*, in reference to Marxist thought, is in English in the original, throughout.—Trans.]

9   "The public" is derived from the Latin word *publicus*. *Publica* means "State income"; the verb *publico*, on the other hand, means to "confiscate, appropriating a common good for the treasury"; *publicum* means a tax, a subsidy, or the place or territory in which the common wealth of the State is located. The *respublica* (or *reipublicae* in the generative) refers in the first place to the "goods of the community"; and, by extension, to all that is common to the community, the locations of communal actions. In Spanish, *público* refers to that which is "known and *seen* by all" (Moliner, *Diccionario del uso del español*, vol. 2, 876).

10 [Here Dussel refers to a series of videos, released publicly in Mexico in recent years, which revealed corrupt transactions involving public officials.—Trans.]

11 See Dussel, *Ética de la liberación*, vol. 1, ch. 1.

12 [In Spanish the verb "to be able" and the noun "power" are represented by the same word, *poder*. This is crucial for a nuanced understanding of the section that follows.—Trans.]

13 [*Encomenderos* were conquistadors entrusted with plantation-like communities (*encomiendas*) based on forced indigenous (and African slave) labor.—Trans.]

14 See Dussel, *Política de la liberación*, vol. 1, 114–19.

15 In German, *Beruf*—which can mean "profession" (*Beruf*) or, in another form, "vocation" (*Berufnung*)—is an ambiguous word, and Weber plays on this ambiguity.

16 We will see that this usage of "must" has a normative character [» 9].

17 In Latin, *ob* means having someone or something "in front" and *audire* means to hear, to listen, to pay attention. The content of "obedience," then, is the act of "knowing how to listen to the other."

18 "Government" comes from the Greek verb *gobernao*, which means to pilot a ship. "Governors" are thus elected pilots, not merely the administrative or bureaucratic body of political society [» 8].

19 The "political justice claim" is to politics what the "goodness claim" is to ethics. It is the honest intention of those who fulfill the *noble vocation of politics*.

20 In Greek this word is διακονός or *diakonós* (in Hebrew עֶבֶד: *hebed*), meaning "the servant."

21 Mark 10:43–44. With these words the founder of Christianity forcefully corrects the corrupt spirit of his disciples.

22 Mark 10:42.

23 [This is *hecho* in Spanish and in Portuguese, and Dussel proceeds to note that "h" and "f" are often interchangeable, as with the Spanish *fechoría* (misdeed) and the island of Formosa, which has its origins in the Spanish *hermosa* (beautiful).—Trans.]

24 "Thus I wish it, thus I order it [says the government]; the will takes the place of *reason*" [Juvenal, *Satires*, vi, 223.—Trans.].That is to say, what I decide should be done *with regard to* what I want. "My desire" is the *foundation* (the *reason*) by which the citizen is obligated.

25 That is, the government can dare to issue laws, but these laws must at least maintain the character of decisions that can be modified.

26 Marx refers to the Semitic text in Psalm 115:4–6: "Their idols are silver and gold, *the work of men's hands*. They have mouths, but they speak not: eyes have they, but they see not: They have ears, but they hear not."

27 Or elected organs that are subordinate to the King.

28 Marx, "On the Assembly of the Estates," 146–47.

29 "Personifizierung der Sache und Versachlichung der Person" (second draft of *Capital*, 1861–1863, notebook 21), in Marx, "Economic Manuscripts of 1861–1863," 123.

30 Marx, "Economic Manuscripts of 1861–1863," 122. [This citation and the one preceding it are also available in Marx, *Theories of Surplus Value*, 389–90. However, the Soviet translation is nearly useless—as, for example, here translating *Verkehrung* as "perversion" rather than as "inversion" or "reversal" (*Marx-Engels Werke*, vol. 26, part 2, 365).—Trans.]

31 This is in the Latin text that Marx cites—*stat pro ratione voluntas*—if we understand that "reason" is the foundation, in the sense of having a "reason" to do or to think something, as the expression of the *rational foundation* demanded by the occasion. The "will" of the representative becomes the "foundation," or the "sufficient reason" of Heidegger.

32 Since the people [» 11], having elected the representatives, believe (and here we see the effect of the faulty interpretation of fetishism as the phenomenal mechanism of semantic inversion) that these representatives are in their delegation and that they are responsible for their acts.

33 As efficient cause: the passive *people* choose the candidates put forward by the powerful elites.

34 This is because fetishized power—be it of the elite or of the liberal or imperial State—claims to be at the "service" of the people, and yet it does so always through first accomplishing its own interests. For instance, when G. W. Bush lowers taxes on the rich so that they can create more jobs, this contributes to the mirage of a "minimal State" that cannot even help the African Americans of New Orleans, because such salvage operations now belong to private initiative and not to a minimal, nonbenefactor State. This is an *inverted* republicanism, which demands the weakening of the State in the name of the community but is in fact a weakening of both the State and the community in favor of the richest. The big business of the bourgeoisie is the exploitation of the poor and the State. The latter can be achieved, for example, through war and the destruction of a country (like Iraq), and by afterward demanding that the very same American State reconstruct it through transnationals with ties to political power (fetishized, and moreover nepotistic, as in the case of the vice president).

35 The eagle, symbol of empires (the Roman, the Nazi, the American), is the king of birds and strikes like lightning *from above* to seize the people with its deadly talons and to seize the fertile earth, the *serpent*, Coatlicue, the *woman* of the agricultural peoples dominated by the Aztec Empire (also represented by an eagle).

36 But history will demand an explanation for the unjust treatment being suffered by the Palestinians, how it comes to pass under a scorched-earth policy, entailing the extinction of entire populations and the enforcement of "an eye for an eye," the savage and barbaric rule that was applied *prior to the emergence of the juridical*

codices of Babylon and prior to the existence of judges and to avoid justice being done "by one's own hands."

37 Sun Tzu, *The Art of War*, ch. 5, 22.

38 Weber, *Economy and Society*, 53.

39 In a second moment, the *"obediential* power" of the leader will demand that the community obey *itself* (insofar as the community has passed these laws and elected representatives, which does not mean that they are not revocable) by fulfilling the just decisions of those who exercise institutional power through *delegation.*

40 See Derrida, *The Politics of Friendship.*

41 For Rancière this is a *political* and not merely a *police* relation (the latter of which would be a relation of domination).

42 The unanimity of direct democracy is a postulate of political reason: ideally or logically conceivable but empirically *impossible.* It was possible in small societies, in Phoenicia or Greece, and in Venice or Calvin's Geneva, but it is no longer feasible in communities consisting of millions of citizens. This does not, how-ever, negate the increasing organization of participation [» 19, 20].

43 See Laclau, *On Populist Reason.*

44 This includes even Jacobo Arbenz, whose toppling by the U.S. Department of State in 1954 and subsequent replacement with the dictatorship of Castillo Armas marked the end of this historical era (along with the coup d'etat against Sukarno in Indonesia and the later fall of Nasser in Egypt).

45 Arendt, *The Human Condition*, 179.

46 Gramsci, *The Prison Notebooks*, 32.

47 Here, Gramsci should have written *"governing* class," because a class is *dominant* only after losing consensus, not *before.* [Dussel refers to the original Italian, which uses the term "dominante" where the English translation gives, in accor-dance with his concern, "ruling."—Trans.]

48 Those rights indicated as civil in reality are meant to respect the full possibility for the citizen to perform tasks in other fields. Subjective rights also recognize faculties or capacities of the subject prior to or following the actor's entry into the political field. The subject is not only a citizen, but also a head of family, a factory worker, a member of a religious organization or soccer club, etc. All of these dimensions are considered as subjective, individual, and civil rights.

49 This is the case since they are always the "conditioned" outgrowth of prior action or of another institution.

50 Once instituted, they "condition" all future action, which becomes a "function" or fulfillment of a determined objective.

51 This worker is obligated to labor to create surplus value out of the void of

capital. This creation of "more value" represents "less life" for the worker—that is, less satisfaction and more pain. The law obligates the worker to fulfill an unjust system. In this case, the political institution represses and kills. The bourgeois revolution in England first organized the disciplinary institutions of liberalism, then carried out the Industrial Revolution, and with both systems—in the political and economic fields—imposed *obedience* on the workers under the threat of unemployment or prison.

52 In my *Ethics of Liberation* ([*Ética de la liberación*] chapters 1 and 4), I discuss this subject in more depth.

53 Derrida, *The Politics of Friendship*.

54 The Supreme Court or Constitutional Tribunal in the final instance, which should equally judge the constitutionality of laws and institutions as well as judging the appearance of *new rights* (through the struggles for recognition of social movements) and the need for a constitutional *modification*.

55 This anticipates questions that I will deal with in part 2, and it is a novelty of the Bolivarian Constitution of Venezuela (1999) [» 20.2].

56 I recently completed my *Politics of Liberation* (*Política de la Liberación*, 2006), in which—through the course of three long volumes—I lay out this thematic in greater detail. The historical portion of this work is forthcoming from Trotta in Madrid.

57 Samir Amin argues that in Egypt the State existed from at least five thousand years ago, since the first dynasties of the Pharaohs, with their dominant classes, tribute systems, and writing that allowed the recording of events, legal codes, etc. Enrique Florescano similarly shows the early origin of the State in the Mayan world, for example, with regard to the theogonic figure of the kings.

58 As when a member of the U.S. Department of State declares that Hugo Chávez could have been elected by a majority, noting that the same occurred with Hitler. In this way, the Empire appropriates the right to evaluate all democratic processes. If the elected is submissive to the external Will-to-Power then he or she is declared to be *truly* democratic, whereas if the elected responds to the people by exercising obediential power (and as a result not obeying the Empire) then he or she is declared *undemocratic*.

59 What televised images determine to be "evil" or "unjust" (which always represents a certain degree of *interpretation*) is imposed on the spectator as *reality itself*. The best politician can be completely *destroyed* by the communication media.

60 See my *Ética de la liberación*.

61 [Here Dussel refers to the fact that, in Spanish, adjectives are given gendered endings to match those of the nouns they modify.—Trans.]

62 One can experiment with the other possibilities. For example, *arrow b* indicates the material determination of feasibility. As an instance, a poor country ("Defend the

life of the people!") cannot have a technically powerful offensive army, but it can develop a defensive tactic that allows it to defeat a better army ("Choose what is feasible!"). Was this not the case of the Spanish people against Napoleon at the beginning of the nineteenth century, or of Iraq against G. W. Bush in 2006?

63 Fichte, *El Estado comercial cerrado*, book 1, chapter 1, ii.

64 The short-term view of four to six years for the exercise of executive power has corrupted national and international politics, such that a project for the survival of humanity during the next thousand years—which would be perfectly feasible —is unthinkable.

65 See my *Política de la liberación*, vol. 2, 24.1.

66 Rousseau, *The Social Contract and Discourse on the Origin of Inequality*, 17–18.

67 See my *Ética de la liberación*, ch. 2.

68 See my *Política de la liberación*, vol. 2, 25.

69 Hegel, *Elements of the Philosophy of Right*, 277 (258).

70 Hinkelammert, *Crítica de la razón utópica*, 22.

71 The political principle of feasibility is contained within the horizon delimited by the first two normative political principles, and it operates to determine the possibility of the goals (it fixes limits *negatively*: "You should not do this because it is *empirically impossible!*"). However, the principle of feasibility exercises a specific action of its own in judging those means, not only as formally fulfilling the goals in question (through the formal rationality described by Weber) but also materially and procedurally with regard to the intrinsic consistency of the means as normative ("Use this means because it affirms life, it is legitimate, and efficient toward the goal!"). One should not torture one's political opponent so that they might *betray* their strategy. This normative-political *impossibility* of torture shows that not all methods are *possible* (to use, judge, determine) for the (normative) ends of politics. The objection can be approximated as follows: "What use is a normativity that reduces strategic possibilities?" The response would be that in the short term it might seem to reduce the possibilities, but in the medium term and the long term it gives coherence while avoiding contradictions, it allows for a firm foundation from which to convince a group of actors, it creates legitimacy, it avoids material conflicts, it allows the actors an honest political justice claim, and it gives actions, institutions, and the political order generally greater permanence, governability, and stability. In sum, such an approach reinforces the *power* (as *potentia* and *potestas*) to allow the achievement of the power-to-create means that are fully accepted by *all citizens*.

72 The notion of unintentional negative effects will be the point of departure for part 2 of this work.

73 See Laclau, *On Populist Reason*.

74 See my *Política de la Liberación*, vol. 3, sec. 36–40.

75 See de Sousa Santos, *El milenio huérfano*.

76 See "The Popular Question," in my *La Producción teórica de Marx*, sec. 18.2, 400.

77 Here Castro recognizes the importance of the singular subject in leading the political process of constructing a people.

78 As such, these are not wage workers—they cannot reproduce their lives; they are Marx's *pauper ante festum*, the marginal, the lumpen.

79 Note here the use of a metaphor rooted in the popular religious imaginary, which was "not very *orthodox*" for a Marxist at that time (although by the time of Evo Morales it would be an obvious example, having been used by Tupac Amaru, Morelos, the Sandinistas, etc.).

80 Castro Ruz, *History Will Absolve Me*.

81 See Lenkersdorf, *Filosofar en clave tojolbal*.

82 Hardt and Negri, *Multitude*, 79.

83 See also my *Philosophy of Liberation*, 2.

84 Marx, "Economic and Philosophical Manuscripts of 1844," 284–85. [The translation was altered by Dussel.—Trans.]

85 Hardt and Negri, in *Multitude*, opt to eliminate sovereignty and authority as determinations proper to the coercive State. Against this, these concepts need to be situated within the political community, and now within the people properly speaking. The sovereign and last reference point for authority is the people itself.

86 Schmitt, *La defensa de la constitución*.

87 See Agamben, *Stato di eccezione*.

88 Zapata, "Plan de Ayala," 404.

89 On critical ethical principles, see Dussel, *Ética de la liberación*, part 2.

90 Marx, "Reflections of a Young Man on the Choice of a Profession," 8.

91 Marx, "Theses on Feuerbach," 143.

92 "We Enter Once Again into History," message from the Ejército Zaporista de Liberación Nacional in *La Jornada*, Mexico City, February 22, 1994, 8.

93 Who today has an acceptable *theory* of socialism, after the ideological crisis of the Soviet bloc?

94 Luxemburg, *Reform or Revolution*.

95 See his *The Principle of Hope*.

96 See my *Ética de la liberación*, chapter 6.1: "The *Question of Organization*: From Vanguard to Symmetrical Participation: Theory and Praxis?"

97 Luxemburg, "Leninism or Marxism?" 102–3.

98 Walzer, *Exodus and Revolution*, 149.

99 This refers to the clay feet—the moment of weakness—of the iron and bronze statue described by the prophet Ezekiel in Semitic thought.

100 I say "ambiguous" because in the Semitic symbolic narrative Joshua is a *conqueror* who needs to kill Canaanites, destroy Jericho, and "cleanse" the earth and occupy it. In sum, this is an unjust action, full of violence and domination. This is the bible that the Americans carried under their arms in the occupation of the "land," the far west, belonging to the Mexicans (the "new Canaanites" in the words of Texan Chicano thinker Virgilio Elizondo) and the Indians.

101 Marx, "Theses on Feuerbach" (3, 11), 144–45. [The translation was altered by Dussel.—Trans.]

102 The first works by Laclau were concerned with demonstrating the error of these diagnostics that suppressed the political field in favor of the necessary laws of the economy. This was a revolutionary, utopian, anti-political economism (utopian in the sense of attempting to carry out empirically that which is impossible, as I will show below in my discussion of postulates).

103 The paradigm or model of a political system is not a short-term, concrete political project.

104 This is "materialist" in the sense indicated, that is: the final *content* of all human acts is the production, reproduction, and improvement of the empirical, immediate, and concrete life of the human being.

105 Engels, "Preface to the First Edition," in *The Origin of the Family, Private Property, and the State*, 71 [The translation was altered by Dussel.—Trans.]. These three requirements for the basic needs of life can be found in chapter 125 of the Egyptian *Book of the Dead* (3000 B.C.) and in the story of the Judgment of the founder of Christianity (Matthew 25:35). See my *Ética de la liberación*, 405.

106 We will see that, on the formal level of democratic legitimacy, Kant proposed the postulate of "perpetual peace." I am extending this working hypothesis analogically to all spheres or politics (material, formal, feasibility).

107 In the future, these ecological costs will be greater than all other production costs.

108 "The universality of man manifests itself in practice in that universality which makes the whole of nature his inorganic body, (1) as a direct means of life and (2) as the matter, the object, and the tool of his life activity. . . . Man lives *from nature*—i.e., nature *is his body*" (Marx, "Economic and Philosophical Manuscripts of 1844," 275–76).

109 That is, it is a postulate: logically thinkable, empirically impossible, a criterion for practical orientation.

110 This is in socialism as well, and even in another, later, and more *developed* system that might be organized.

111 This rationalization can in no way be a *perfect* planning, as the latter was a false postulate of real socialism, because not only is it empirically impossible but it also is oriented toward a negation of the market that is unnecessary and destroys

it to greater negative effect. Planning should be at a minimal and necessary level to complete the requirements that Marx explains below.

112   This "control" suggests a prudent intervention in the market, toward the indicated criterion.

113   [I have found it necessary here to cut a portion of the Soviet translation, as it was inaccurate and would only obscure Dussel's point.—Trans.]

114   The criterion is the "minimal employment" of labor, of human life.

115   Here, the normative principles of economics and politics enter into play, setting out from the *dignity of human nature*, the absolute criterion of all normativity. Marx judges facts according to normative principles and orienting postulates.

116   That is, the postulate understands empirically its own *impossibility* as concrete reality, but it is nonetheless formulated as an orienting criterion (a "regulative idea").

117   Marx, *Capital*, vol. 3, 799–800.

118   The ecological problem is not a technological one (of pollution); rather, it is an economic problem of capital. The criterion of increasing relative surplus-value consists in implementing better technology in order to reduce the value of the singular product, which through *competition* lowers prices and displaces opponent capitals. But the criterion of technological subsumption in the productive process is not ecological (the best technology for "perpetual life" on Earth) but rather economically capitalist (the immediate decrease in the value of the product). Those technologies that are destructive of ecology are the result of this deadly criterion that destroys life: namely, competition between individual capitals under the demand for an increased rate of profit. This is economic, not technological. See my *Las metáforas teológicas de Marx*, 224. Marx is an excellent theorist of ecology.

119   The liberal political *system* (in the political field) leaves to the *historical institution of the market* (part of the capitalist system, in the economic field) all economic responsibility, and it rejects, at least in theory, the utility of political intervention in that system (and field). The market, as a structure of knowledge for Hayek, and as a result of the "wise" and natural laws of competition, creates equilibrium and resolves economic problems by itself. The politician, according to Smith, should not have the arrogance to stick his or her "hand" into this sphere (only the providential "hand of God" has this right).

120   The idea is that all citizens, for the fact of being citizens, receive an income that allows them to live. This possibility has been studied in detail. See Gilbert and Raventos, "El subsidio universal garantizado: Notas para continuar."

121   Hinkelammert and Mora, *Hacia una economía para la vida*. See especially "Toward a Theory of the Value-of-Human-Life" (chapter 13.5, 377).

122 See Razeto Migliaro, *Empresas de trabajadores y economía de mercado* and *Economía de solidaridad y mercado democrático*; Coraggio, *La gente o el capital*; and Hinkelammert and Duchrow, *La vida o el capital*.

123 [Dussel refers here to *La Malinche*, an indigenous woman who according to legend gave birth to the Mestizo nation through her relationship with Cortés. As a result she is presented as having been anything from a victim to a traitor.—Trans.]

124 Secular Modernity rejects the value of non-European religions, and even the Enlightenment, upon producing a secularist ideology, destroyed the very nucleus of Latin American, African, and Asian cultures that existed prior to and alongside the deployment of Modernity. Secularism was equally a coercive instrument, because religious narratives often constitute the fundamental ethical-mythical nucleus of the great postcolonial cultures of the periphery.

125 He refers to the method of the prophets of Israel, concretely, as a political method.

126 Cohen, *Religion der Vernunft aus den Quellen des Judentums*, prologue.

127 In the manner already indicated, in which the representative affirms him or herself as the center of power [» 5] and not as one who exercises *delegated* power in an *obediential* manner [» 4].

128 Or what we in Latin America know as a municipality.

129 See Arendt, *On Revolution*.

130 *Arrow a* in figure 13 indicates the management of delegated power in the representative institutions. *Arrow b*, on the other hand, shows the management of control (even including the revocation of mandates) of representatives. This would avoid the fetishism of party bureaucracies.

131 "Freedom of the press" defends a right of the media against the State, and it has done so since the end of the eighteenth century. The "right to truthful information" defends the citizen against mediaocracy: it is a *new* right.

132 Thus moving from *potestas* to *potentia*, and from the *singular* to the *plural*, from the "L'État c'est moi!" (The king of France's phrase, "I am the State!") to "We are the State!"

133 In the near future, it will be possible to have in a matter of seconds the opinions of the totality of the citizenry on some urgent question, thanks to the use of cell phones and computers that can reveal the position of *all* members of the community, the people. The electronic revolution is the equivalent of the industrial revolution of the eighteenth century! But while the latter principally effected the process of industrial production, the former also intervenes in the process of making political decisions and informing the citizens about *all* actions of the government, in part as a "community of networks." For Hardt and Negri, the

electronically informed "multitude" is opposed to the "people." However, while I am not in agreement with these authors, it is clear that the people, too—in order to increase strategic feasibility, to accelerate the coordination of its action and defense against repression—need to be constituted in a *community of networks*, as occurs in the World Social Forum or in the Zapatista movement. The poor are increasingly empowered every day thanks to electronic media, which allow a broadened solidarity, from the local to the national or the global.

134 *Participation* needs to be generalized in all institutions: student participation in the universities and educational institutions, workers in factories, of the members, spectators, and players in sports clubs (even on the highest level), of reporters in television, newspapers, radio, etc. A *participatory* society, in which citizens are *actors*, could be politically democratic and self-managed.

135 Sen, *Bienestar, justicia y mercado.*

136 See my *Hacia una filosofía política crítica*, 145.

137 The use of "critical" refers to the moment in which the political actor has lost the naiveté of thinking that the existing system, for the mere fact of existing, is already just. In seeing the system from the perspective of the oppressed and excluded, the political actor gains a deconstructive "critical" consciousness and offers to transform that system insofar as is necessary. This is a *"critical* and political aspiration to justice"—namely, material, formal, and feasible *justice* (in a broader sense than even that indicated by MacIntyre in *Whose Justice? Which Rationality?*).

138 See *Tratado por el que se establece una Constitución para Europa.* I am not referring to the use that the transnationals make of this confederation against the achievements of two centuries of social struggles.

The works of Enrique Dussel can also be consulted on the Internet at http://www.enriquedussel.org

Agamben, Giorgio. *Stato di eccezione*. Turin: Bollati Boringhieri, 2003.

Arendt, Hannah. *The Human Condition*. New York: Doubleday, 1958.

——. *On Revolution*. New York: Viking, 1963.

Bloch, Ernst. *The Principle of Hope*. Cambridge: MIT Press, 1995.

Bourdieu, Pierre. "Champ." In *Questions de Sociologie*. Paris: Minuit, 1984.

——. *L'ontologie politique de Martin Heidegger*. Paris: Minuit, 1989.

——. *Les règles de l'art: Genèse et structure du champ littéraire*. Paris: Minuit, 1992.

——. "The Uses of People." In *In Other Words*. Cambridge, England: Polity, 1990.

Castells, Manuel. *The Information Age: Economy, Society, and Culture*. Vol. 1: *The Rise of the Network Society*. Mexico City: Siglo XXI, 1996.

Castro Ruz, Fidel. *History Will Absolve Me*. Trans. P. Álvarez and A. Booth, 1953. Available at the Web site of the Marxist Internet Archive.

Clausewitz, Karl von. *On War*. New York: Penguin, 1968.

Cohen, Hermann. *Religion der Vernunft aus den Quellen des Judentums*. Darmstadt: Melzer, 1919.

Coraggio, José Luis. *La gente o el capital: Desarrollo local y economía del trabajo*. Buenos Aires: Espacio Editorial, 2004.

Derrida, Jacques. *The Politics of Friendship*. London: Verso, 2006.

De Sousa Santos, Boaventura. *El milenio huérfano: Ensayos para una nueva cultura política*. Madrid: Trotta, 2005.

Dussel, Enrique. *Etica de la liberación*. Madrid: Trotta, 1998.

——. *Hacia una filosofía política crítica*. Bilbao: Desclée de Brouwer, 2001.

——. *Hacia una política de la liberación*. Madrid: Plaza y Valdés, 2007.

——. *Las metáforas teológicas de Marx*. Estella: Verbo Divino, 1993.

——. *Philosophy of Liberation*. New York: Orbis, 1989.

——. *Política de la liberación*. Madrid: Trotta, 2007.

——. *La producción teórica de Marx: Una introducción a los "Grundrisse."* Mexico City: Siglo XXI, 1985.

Engels, F. *The Origin of the Family, Private Property, and the State*. New York: International Publishers, 1972.

Fichte, Johan Gottlieb. *El Estado comercial cerrado*. Madrid: Tecnos, 1991.

Freire, Paolo. *Pedagogy of the Oppressed*. New York: Continuum, 2000.

Gilbert, R., and D. Raventos. "El subsidio universal garantizado: Notas para continuar." *Mientras tanto* (Barcelona), winter 1966–67.

Gramsci, Antonio. *The Prison Notebooks*, vol. 2, ed. J. A. Buttigieg. New York: Columbia University Press, 1975.

Hardt, Michael, and Antonio Negri. *Multitude: War and Democracy in the Age of Empire*. New York: Penguin, 2004.

Hegel, G. W. F. *Elements of the Philosophy of Right*. Trans. H. B. Nisbet. Cambridge: Cambridge University Press, 1991.

Hinkelammert, Franz. *Crítica de la razón utópica*. San José, Costa Rica: Departamento Ecuménico de Investigaciones, 1984.

Hinkelammert, Franz, and U. Duchrow. *La vida o el capital: Alternativas a la dictadura global de la propiedad*. Mexico City: Dríada, 2004.

Hinkelammert, Franz, and H. Mora. *Hacia una economía para la vida*. San José, Costa Rica: Departamento Ecuménico de Investigaciones, 2005.

Horkheimer, Max. *Critique of Instrumental Reason*. London: Continuum, 1983.

Laclau, Ernesto. *On Populist Reason*. London: Verso, 2005.

Lenkersdorf, Carlos. *Filosofar en clave tojolbal*. Mexico City: Miguel Angel Porrúa, 2002.

Levinas, Emmanuel. *Otherwise than Being or Beyond Essence*. Boston: Martines Nijhoff, 1981.

———. *Totality and Infinity: An Essay on Exteriority*. Pittsburgh: Duquesne University Press, 1969.

Luhmann, Niklas. *Poder*. Barcelona: Anthropos, 1995.

———. *Die Politik der Gesellschaft*. Frankfurt: Suhrkamp, 2000.

Luxemburg, Rosa. "Leninism or Marxism?" In *The Russian Revolution and Leninism or Marxism?* Ann Arbor: University of Michigan Press, 1961.

———. *Reform or Revolution*. 1900. Available at the Web site of the Marxist Internet Archive.

MacIntyre, Alasdair. *Whose Justice? Which Rationality?* Notre Dame: University of Notre Dame Press, 1988.

Marx, Karl. *Capital*. Moscow: Foreign Languages, 1962.

———. "Economic and Philosophical Manuscripts of 1844." In *Karl Marx, Frederick Engels: Collected Works*, vol. 3. New York: International Publishers, 1975.

———. "Economic Manuscripts of 1861–1863." In *Karl Marx, Frederick Engels: Collected Works*, vol. 34. New York: International Publishers, 1975.

———. *Karl Marx–Friedrich Engels Gesamtausgabe*. Berlin: Dietz, 1975.

——. *Marx-Engels Werke*, vol. I. Berlin: Dietz, 1956.

——. "Proceeding of the Sixth Rhine Province Assembly." In *Karl Marx, Frederick Engels: Collected Works*, vol. I. New York: International Publishers, 1975.

——. "Reflection of a Young Man on the Choice of a Profession." In *Karl Marx, Frederick Engels: Collected Works*, vol. I. New York: International Publishers, 1975.

——. *Theories of Surplus Value*, part I. Moscow: Progress, 1963.

——. "Theses on Feuerbach." In *The Marx-Engels Reader*, ed. R. Tucker. New York: W. W. Norton, 1978.

Meadows, Donella, et al. *The Limits to Growth*. New York: Universe, 1972.

Moliner, María. *Diccionario del uso del español*. 2 vols. Madrid: Gredos, 1992.

Razeto Migliaro, Luis. *Economía de solidaridad y mercado democrático*. Santiago, Chile: Programa de Economía del Trabajo, 1985.

——. *Empresas de trabajadores y economía de mercado*. Santiago, Chile: Programa de Economía del Trabajo, 1982.

Rousseau, Jean-Jacques. *The Social Contract and Discourse on the Origin of Inequality*, ed. L. Crocker. New York: Washington Square, 1967.

Schmitt, Carl. *La defensa de la constitución*. Madrid: Tecnos, 1998.

Sen, Amartya. *Bienestar, justicia y mercado*. Barcelona: Paidos, 1998.

Sun Tzu. *El arte de la guerra*, ed. Albert Galvany. Madrid: Trotta, 2001.

Tratado por el que se establece una Constitución para Europa. Madrid: Biblioteca Nueva, Real Instituto Elcano, 2004.

Walzer, Michael. *Exodus and Revolution*. New York: Basic Books, 1985.

Weber, Max. *Economy and Society: An Outline of Interpretive Sociology*. Berkeley: University of California Press, 1978.

Force, 32, 40–42, 79, 102, 103–4
Foucault, Michel, xii, 27, 46
Fraternity, 38, 47–49; solidarity vs., 137.
  See also Revolution, bourgeois
Freud, Sigmund, 46
Friends, 38–39, 49, 81, 121. See also
  Enemies
Fujimori, Alberto, xvii

Globalization, vii, 96
Governability, 54, 133, 135–38; symmetry
  and, 135
Government, 140 n. 18; by law, 51–53, 82,
  104
Gramsci, Antonio, 40–42, 44–45, 54, 75,
  98–99, 103–4, 133, 142 n. 47
Guevara, Che, 25

Habermas, Jürgen, 50, 56, 66, 80, 89
Hayek, Friedrich von, 116, 147 n. 119
Hegel, G. W. F., 19, 67
Hegemony, 39–41; analogical hegemon,
  73–75; crisis of, 79–80, 103–4 (see also
  Praxis: anti-hegemonic); new, 81, 106–7
Heidegger, Martin, 13, 121
Hellenism, xi, 124
Hidalgo, Miguel, 25, 81, 92, 104–5
Hinkelammert, Franz, 48, 63, 67
Hitler, Adolf, xvii, 33, 143 n. 58
Hobbes, Thomas, 13, 15, 32, 44, 60
Holocaust, 35, 80
Horkheimer, Max, 53, 84, 94, 97
Hurricane Katrina, 141 n. 34
Husserl, Edmund, 8
Hyperpotentia, 76, 78–82, 90, 94, 106

Impossiblility, possible logically. See Pos-
  tulate, political
Inclusion, 89
Information, 129–30

Instincts, 13, 46
Institutionalization of power. See Potestas
Institutions: of feasibility, 46, 53–55, 131–
  38; institutional spheres (level B) 36,
  43–55; of legitimacy or democracy, 46,
  50–51, 122–30; material, 43–49, 114–21;
  political, 7–8, 17–20, 36
International Monetary Fund, vii, xiii, 33, 82
Intersubjectivity, 5–6, 8–9, 43, 65, 71; liberation praxis and, 98, 126
Iraq, 35, 122; resistance in, 82, 91, 106, 144
  n. 62
Isaac, 58

Jefferson, Thomas, 128
Joan of Arc, 25
Joshua, 106, 146 n. 100
Justice, 91–93, 135–38

Kant, Immanuel, x, 32, 38–39, 44, 51, 56,
  63, 112, 146 n. 106
Keynesian economics, 96
Kirchner, Nestor, xv, 101
Kissinger, Henry, 25
Kondratieff, Nikolai Dmytriyevich, 110

Laclau, Ernesto, 72–73, 146 n. 102
Las Casas, Bartolomé de, 15
Laws of the Indies (Spain), 105
Legitimacy: compulsion and, 104–6; crit-
  ical, 79–81, 88–89, 105, 122–30
Legitimation, system of, 46, 50–51, 122–30
Lenin, Vladimir, 13, 99
Levels of politics: 36–37; level A, 36–42;
  level B, 43–55; level C, 56–68
Leviathan, 15, 31–33, 44
Leviathan (Hobbes), 60
Levinas, Emmanuel, ix, 78, 81, 121
Liberalism, xvi, 15, 32, 47, 65, 71, 82, 93,
  147 n. 119

Schopenhauer, Arthur, 13
Secularism, 134, 148 n. 124
Sein, 19–20
Sen, Amartya, 135
Service, 27–29. *See also* Politics: as vocation;
    Power: obediential; Representation
Similarity. *See* Analogy
Smith, Adam, 147 n. 119
Social, the, 39, 43–45
Social Contract (Rousseau), 63–64
Socialism, xvi, 32, 47, 65, 71, 116, 127, 145
    n. 93, 146 n. 111
Social movements, 71–73, 75, 98–99, 104,
    107, 125; differential, 39
Society: Civil, 39, 44–45, 54, 75–76, 134;
    Political, 44–45, 54, 75–76, 104–5
Solidarity, 121, 123; versus fraternity, 137
Soros, George, 118
Sousa Santos, Boaventura de, 72–73
Spartacus, 25
Spinoza, Baruch, 20, 60
Spivak, Gayatri, vii
Spontaneism, 27, 64, 127
Stalin, Joseph, 34
State, 131–32 (*see also* Society: Political);
    dissolution of, 132; fetishism of, 3–4;
    liberal-minimal, 46–47, 141 n. 34
State of exception, 82
State of rebellion, 82, 129
Strategic action, 36–42, 94–107; coercive,
    32; hegemonic, 39–40. *See also* Praxis
Strategy, 97
Suárez, Francisco, 21
Subject, 5–6
Subjectified state, 132
Subsumption, analogical. *See* Analogy
Sukarno, 142 n. 44
Sun Tzu, 37–38
Symmetry, 15, 53; democratic, 64–65, 80,

99; governability and, 135. *See also*
Consensus
System, 5, 7–8; capitalist, 48; of law and
    rights, 51–53, 105; new, of law and
    rights 123–26; political, 111–12, 135

Totality, 3, 67; rupture of, 78–79. *See also*
    Praxis: anti-hegemonic
Transformation, 110–12
Trotsky, Leon, 13
Tupac Amaru, 106, 145 n. 79

Utopia, *63*, 96, 100. *See also* Postulate,
    political

Validity. *See* Democracy; Political princi-
    ple, normative
Vanguard, xvi, 105; rearguard vs., 98–99
Vargas, Getúlio, 40, 76
Vázquez, Tabaré, xv, 101
Victims, 69, 78–82, 83–86, 88–90, 121
Vietnam, 91
Violence, 103–6; revolutionary, 111

Wallerstein, Immanuel, 130
Walzer, Michael, 102
War: Clausewitz on, 7; just, 104
Washington, George, 25, 104
Weber, Max, 16, 31, 33, 38, 41, 53, 65, 88,
    144 n. 71
Will: -to-Live, 13, 78, 98; -to-Power, 13,
    33–34, 78, 143 n. 58
World, 5–7
World Bank, vii, xiii, 33, 82
World Social Forum, xv, 39, 96, 106

Young, Iris, 89

Zapata, Emiliano, 83
Zapatismo, *19*, 48, 95, 99, 120, 149 n. 133.
    See also Command: obeying
Zedillo, Ernesto, 120

ENRIQUE DUSSEL teaches philosophy at the Universidad Autónoma Metropolitana, Iztapalapa, and at the Universidad Autónoma de México in Mexico City. He is one of the founders of the philosophy of liberation. Born in Argentina, he has lived in exile in Mexico for more than thirty years. He has published an impressive number of articles and books such as *Philosophy of Liberation* (translated in 1985), *The Invention of the Americas: Eclipse of the "Other" and the Myth of Modernity* (translated in 1995), and *The Underside of Modernity: Apel, Ricoeur, Rorty, Taylor, and the Philosophy of Liberation* (translated in 1996). He has also published a three-volume commentary to the four drafts of Marx's *Capital* (1985–1990), as well as an encyclopedic work on ethical philosophy entitled *Etica de la liberación en la edad de la globalización y la exclusión* (1998). He is currently working on a three-volume work on political philosophy from a liberation philosophy perspective, the first of which was published in Spanish as *Política de la liberación*. *Twenty Theses on Politics* offers a summary of the main theses of these three volumes.

Library of Congress Cataloging-in-Publication Data

Dussel, Enrique D.
[20 tesis de política. English]
Twenty theses on politics / Enrique Dussel ; translated by George Ciccariello-Maher ; foreword by Eduardo Mendieta.
p. cm. — (Latin America in translation)
Includes bibliographical references and index.
ISBN 978-0-8223-4345-5 (cloth : alk. paper) —
ISBN 978-0-8223-4328-8 (pbk. : alk. paper)
1. Political science. 2. Latin America—Politics and government. I. Title.
JA69.S6D8713 2008
320—dc22
2008024945